ISBN 978-0-484-34417-3
PIBN 10086060

A Manual
For Use of Superintendents,
Principals and School
Officials

by

FREDERICK A. WELCH

STATE INSPECTOR GRADED AND
HIGH SCHOOLS

Des Moines, Iowa

W. M. WELCH MANUFACTURING COMPANY
1516 Orleans Street
Chicago, Ill.

PREFACE

This book is not a philosophical treatise on the American School System.   Such books have a valuable place in our educational literature, and a number of excellent books of this nature have recently been written.   Some especially valuable books, also, have been written on "The American High School", showing its purpose, place, etc. I can here do no better service to the readers of this handbook than to urge upon them the use of one or more of these more pretentious volumes.

Nor is this a book of methods.   This field is well covered already, and by authors far better able to write on such a theme.   An aspiring superintendent or principal will familiarize himself with such valuable school literature.   He cannot best gauge his own work nor best assist his teachers without some knowledge of methods of teaching.

The present volume pretends to be no more than its title indicates, a manual for frequent use.   As such, however, it is alone in its field.   It has grown out of the experiences and observations of the author during twenty years as superintendent of village and city schools in communities ranging in population from three hundred to twelve thousand, and during four years as state inspector of village and city schools.   These experiences and observations have been supplemented by frequent conferences with successful superintendents in various sized schools, and by talks with many members of boards of education.

The preparation of this volume has been prompted by the testimony of many principals and superintendents that they have no way of knowing what other schools are doing, and therefore no way of gauging the success of their work.   497580

While a few universities and fewer colleges now offer some work in "School Supervision", there are not yet adequate means for the prospective principal or superintendent to secure training for his profession. His teachers may be well trained for their tasks, but he must yet depend mostly on "the school of experience", which is a long-term school. This book is intended to assist such principals and superintendents, and it is believed that it will also be of decided help to those who are experienced. Here, too, members of boards of education will be enabled in brief space to find just the information they need to understand their problems and to familiarize themselves with the workings of the present school system.

While not all users of this book will agree with the author in every opinion expressed herein, it is the author's desire and belief that the book will constitute a safe working basis, and that it will prove suggestive of more and better ideas lying perhaps dormant in the minds of principals, superintendents and school officials who read its pages. It is intended not only as a book to be once read, but as a handbook to be kept ready at hand to assist in solving the various problems frequently arising, which the possible limited experience of the user cannot assist in solving. Because the author in his early experience in superintending and supervising his school longed for just such assistance but could not get it, he has faith that other young men and young women in the work today will welcome such help. If even one earnest and ambitious young person is helped thereby, the author will feel repaid for the effort in preparing the volume.

In preparation of this volume the author is especially indebted for valuable suggestions to his chief in the office, and to his fellow workers in the Department. He is also indebted to numerous experienced superintendents in the field and to other educators with whom he has from time to time discussed the problems here treated. Especially does the author feel indebted to Dr. J. E. Stout of Northwestern University for valuable suggestions, and to Dr. C. P. Colegrove of Pasadena, California, educator, author and lecturer, for examination of the manuscript.

—F. A. W.

TABLE OF CONTENTS

TABLE OF CONTENTS—Continued

TABLE OF CONTENTS—Continued

INTRODUCTION

A century ago nearly 90% of the population of the United States lived in the country and subsisted by agriculture. Cities were few, communities were isolated, commerce restricted, organizations simple, and nearly all the arts and vocations of the times had their center in the home. The schools of the period grew out of the needs and conditions of a pioneer people. These schools were crude in organization, local in management, ungraded, short-termed, with a three R's course, taught by men, and wholly unsupervised by the state.

With the marvelous era of expansion and invention, the industrial revolution, the rapid growth of cities, the passing of the home as the industrial center, and the increasing complexity of our social organization, the functions of the school were greatly increased and enlarged. Gradually the school has been transformed into a great state and national institution, with a vast capital invested in buildings and equipment, with elaborate courses of study covering twelve years, with a nine months' program of study each year, with a scientific method of instruction, and a vast army of twenty million pupils taught by 650,000 teachers—in short, the biggest and most important business in our republic. The dircetion and management of this immense business have been delegated to school boards, superintendents and principals.

To be even reasonably successful a great business enterprise requires definite objectives, scientific management and wise supervision. No one is capable of such intelligent direction and administration of a great school plant unless he has been adequately trained for such service. This training may be acquired in two ways:

(1) by actual experience; (2) by careful study, observation and scientific investigation.

From the nature of the case the "experience" method was the only one possible at first. While our great city school systems, our universities, our normal colleges, our rural consolidated schools were growing up they had to be administered by men in service who grew up with them. Such men were Horace Mann, W. T. Harris, Philbrick, Angel, Eliot, Harper and Seerley. They studied their problems while the problems were in the making, experimented, proved all things, held fast to the useful and grew into giant stature by meeting according to their best judgment the increasingly complex duties demanded by the expanding institutions under their management. These men, with scores of other school administrators of long service, have established many important principles of supervision, tried out many methods of organization, determined many definite educational facts, tested many fascinating theories. They have, in fact, created a science of school administration and supervision.

Now the management of great school systems and educational institutions must be given over to young men who have had little actual experience in school administration. Unless such men have carefully studied the ideals, the philosophy and the history of our great pioneers in educational practice, they stand helpless and bewildered before the difficult problems that demand a solution. Such a superintendent or principal, powerless to direct, with no definite policy, weak in purpose, erratic in method, is a pitiful figure—an educational tragedy.

To aid the young superintendent and principal in his duties this volume has been written. The author has gathered his material from a long experience as an administrator of schools, a close study of educational reports and several years of field service as a state inspector of graded and high schools, where he has met school officials, face to face, to talk over the betterment of their local educational conditions. From all these sources a large body of vital and approved principles, directions and suggestions have been selected and put into usable form. They are presented in clear, concise and definite language. They are not mere theory and guesswork, but are intensely practical and useful. The careful study of these principles and directions on the part of superintendents and principals of schools cannot fail to prove of immense value to the pupils, the teachers and the communities that they serve.

Not only to the superintendents and principals will this manual be of service, but to the members of boards of education as well—that great body of public spirited citizens serving without compensation in the field of public school education. Here, in concise form, may be found a workable basis for guidance of school officials. Best methods are presented for solving the various problems to be considered by these men and women trusted with local management of schools. Such persons are naturally busy with their own business, social and personal problems, and cannot give intensive study nor extended time to familiarize themselves with various school problems. This manual, in brief space, will lay before them the general field of operation and will give sound advice on questions of local management of schools. School officials, thus, as well as superintendents and principals, should welcome such a volume presented in this brief and concise way.

C. P. COLEGROVE,
Pasadena, California.

CHAPTER I

Historical Development of Our Public Schools

Nature of Our System. The public school system of the United States is unique, both in the nature of development and in its method of government. We have no national or federal system of schools, as do most other countries. Instead, we have a separate system in each state, the forty-eight state systems resembling each other somewhat closely. The public schools are financed by state and local funds, in many states mostly by the latter. However, a few states, among them Texas and California, have such a large state fund for public school maintenance that local taxation for the purpose is extremely low in rate. With the exception of some early national land grants for public schools and the bonus to states for vocational instruction under the recent Smith-Hughes Act, our federal government has no share in financing our public schools.

The general government, however, has been generous in assisting higher education in the states, especially agricultural colleges. The present tendency is to extend similar aid to the secondary part of our public schools and at the same time to exercise some slight control over the work of the schools. In other words, the present tendency is toward more centralization in public school education. No doubt, however, our schools will continue to remain largely under state and local control.

Colonial Schools. In our early history, strange as it may seem, the colonies established colleges and universities before they gave attention to either secondary schools or elementary schools. The colleges were needed to develop ministers for the church and political leaders for village and state. As early as 1636 Harvard University was established in Massachusetts, by General Court. Virginia, by statutory enactment, established William and Mary's College as its first public educational institution in 1692.

The General Court of Massachusetts in 1647 decreed that every township inhabited by fifty householders should appoint some one of its number to teach. This was probably the first legislation for elementary public schools in America. The act of the General Court also required that in every township of one hundred householders a Grammar School should be established to prepare students for college. This was also probably the first legislation in America for a public secondary school.

In Virginia elementary and secondary education were long left to take care of themselves. There were in the South some voluntary elementary schools started, but much of the schooling was by private tutor.

The first academy in the colonies was set up in Philadelphia in 1751. The academy differed from the Latin Grammar School of Massachusetts in that it was privately endowed instead of publicly financed. The academy was religious in its origin and in most part remained so during its history. However, it proved to be more democratic in nature than was the public Latin Grammar School. The Grammar School sought to prepare for college the wealthier and more precocious; the Academy sought to extend its services more to the masses. In general, the latter enrolled the more mature students. The Latin Grammar School did not develop west of the Alleghenies; the Academy spread throughout the Central States. The Latin Grammar School extended downward from college; the Academy extended upward from the elementary school.

High Schools.   The first High School was founded in Boston in 1821, and was called the English Classical School.   This type of school spread rapidly and in time supplanted both the Latin Grammar School and the Academy.   Today, very few academies are found except in connection with the colleges, and colleges are gradually dispensing with the academy course.   The modern High School performs the function both of preparation for college, as did the Latin Grammar School, and the extension of the Elementary School, as did the Academy. In general it may be stated that the Latin Grammar School flourished during the Colonial period to the Revolutionary War, the Academy during the construction period of our Government to the Civil War, and the Public High School during the reconstruction period since the Civil War.

Plans of Organization.   The Public High School usually consists of four years of work following eight years of preparation in an elementary course in the common branches.   The curriculum is almost entirely distinct from that of the elementary school.   In course of study the High School has moved from the classical course and foreign language course of the Latin Grammar School and the early Academy to a more liberal course in History, Science, Commercial and Vocational subjects.   This has called for equipment, laboratories and libraries.   A broader course is offered, and in the larger high schools election of subject matter is provided.

In the past few years a new organization of school is being tried out by a plan known as the Junior-Senior High School, or the 6-3-3 plan.   The elementary grades here have a six-year course and the high school a six-year course, three years of Junior High School and three years of Senior High School.   A modification of this plan is the Elementary-Intermediate-High School plan, or the 6-2-4 plan of six years of elementary work, two years of intermediate work and four years of high school work. Either plan calls for a modification in Course of Study in the Seventh and Eighth grades. These have much promise and are beyond the experimental stage. It is not wise, for several reasons, for the small school to attempt the new plan.

Since in many states colleges and universities are becoming crowded, especially in Freshman and Sophomore years, a few city high schools are extending the course to include two years of college work. If this plan extends to numerous city high schools it will both solve the problem of congestion in colleges and universities, and at the same time, because of proximity of the students to the school, make it possible for more students to receive at least two years of college work. There is an opinion by some that such work ought to receive a subsidy from the state.

Still another plan being suggested is that the school should be organized as follows: Elementary, six years; Grammar School or Junior High School, two years; High School proper, three years, and Junior College, three years, including two years of college work. This would simply be a change in organization. By this plan it is thought more students would pursue the Junior College work, since they would enter this department one year earlier.

CHAPTER II

School Officials and Their Functions

In the management of the school we have several factors, or agents, the Board of Education, the superintendent, the high school principal and often one or more principals of ward schools. In the small school there are usually no ward principals, and sometimes the superintendent performs also the function of high school principal. ·

Board of Education. The Board of Education, numbering ordinarily from five to nine members, is usually elected by the people of the district, although a few of the larger cities, such as Chicago, have an appointive plan. Usually all board members are chosen at large, and do not represent any particular ward, or district. This is a legislative body in general, although it has some executive and also some judicial functions. The "Board" is also custodian of all the school property. A secretary, or clerk, is generally chosen from outside the "Board".

It is the duty of the Board of Education to provide a plant and equipment for the school, to establish a school year and to fix upon a course of study. Perhaps one of the most important duties of the Board of Education is to elect the superintendent, principals and teachers. In the smaller districts most of these duties are performed by the "Board" acting together as a whole. Some of the larger districts, however, have numerous committees, with which are left the performance of most of the duties. A few of the committees provided are, finance, buildings and grounds, supplies, or purchasing committee, education, and teachers' committee. Usually a committee consists of three members appointed by the president of the "Board". The first named committeeman acts as chairman. While some duties may perhaps be better performed by a special or a standing committee, the tendency seems to be to overdo the committee appointments. Some duties, such as shaping a course of study and electing a superintendent, principals and teachers are surely important enough to engross the attention of the whole "Board". In the ordinary district there seems no warrant for committees other than a purchasing committee and a committee on buildings and grounds.

Other duties of the "Board" are to estimate levies for school purposes and to direct the taking of the annual census of children of school age. Boards should, and in most cases do, hold regular monthly board meetings. The better schools require the superintendent to attend all regular board meetings, to give a general report on the progress of the school, and to make needed recommendations. This is very important. It is a means of keeping the members of the "Board" in close touch with the plans of the school, and at the same time it adds to the superintendent the important responsibility of keeping himself fully informed on all departments of the work of the school. In meeting the superintendent in this way, however, the "Board" should be careful not to overawe him, nor to hamper him in his plans. In general, his recommendations should be adopted, unless good reasons appear for contrary action. There should always in these meetings be co-operation and a spirit of frankness.

The Superintendent. The superintendent is elected by and is an agent of the Board of Education. He is more than the latter, however, as he shapes educational policies and supervises the work of principals and teachers. He should nominate principals and teachers for election, and when they are elected, he should assign them to their department of the work.

With the advice of the "Board", the superintendent shapes the course of study and directs the general educational policy of the school. He should be a strong leader for his teachers and should be able to train them in service. He is also the first "court of appeal" for pupils, teachers and patrons. The custom in a few districts is for pupils, teachers and patrons to take their grievances directly to some member of the Board of Education, without first seeking relief and adjustment in the superintendent's office. This is both unfair to the superintendent and disastrous to the school. Board members may easily prevent this by requiring these matters first to be presented to the superintendent. If they can not here be satisfactorily adjusted, the aggrieved party may be permitted to present the matter to the "Board" in session, but not to individual members of that body.

Aside from such specific duties within the school, the superintendent has some important general duties. He should be in touch with the business and social interests of the community, and participate in a reasonable and legitimate way in such activities. As far as possible, he ought to become acquainted with the parents of the pupils. A study should be made of the future needs of the school, so that at the proper time provision may be made for supplying these needs. The superintendent, to be of most worth, should be a strong community leader, and represent the school in a public way.

The superintendent needs to be a very strong organizer. Much of his success depends on his ability to organize. He must at the same time be an administrator of affairs within the school and a director of certain activities without the school. Perhaps the greatest lack in the average superintendent of schools is his inability or disinclination properly to supervise the work of the teachers and to co-ordinate the work of the various departments. Some experienced teachers in the school system may need very little supervision in their work, while other inexperienced teachers need much help. It is the superintendent's duty to ascertain the department needing assistance and to find time to render such.

Ward Principals. What has been said regarding the duties of the superintendent will, in a slight way, apply to ward principals. They bear the same relation to their district, the parents, the pupils and the teachers, but do not have direct relations with the Board of Education. They direct and supervise the work of their teachers, but have no direct part in choosing them nor complete authority in assigning them to their positions. In their school they are direct agents of the superintendent. Usually the ward principals spend a part of their time in instruction.

The High School Principal. The high school principal has a similar relation to the superintendent and to the Board of Education as do the ward principals, but he has a wider constituency. In his work he is more of a specialist than either the ward principals or the superintendent. The high school is the most complex part of the school organization. The high school principal cannot deal with his students through his teachers only, but in their activities and organizations he must deal with them directly. He must be tactful in directing all the agencies of his school so as to grant freedom of action to all adolescent youth and yet keep a constraining hand on their actions. Whatever is done by the organizations of his school should be under the control of the school.

It is also a difficult matter to properly finance the activities of the high school. In all this the high school must be an integral part of the whole school system and work in harmony with it. The high school principal, also, has no direct relations with the Board of Education, but is responsible directly to the superintendent. In small and moderate-sized high schools the principal usually teaches one or more classes. Where his time permits him to do so it is wise, for he is thus better acquainted with the student body and in closer touch with the actual work of the school. In this way he is also better able to keep the student attitude.

General Considerations. A few general considerations are in point at this time. While the system calls for responsibility to those higher in authority and demanding of fealty on the part of those lower in authority, there should be on the part of all factors and agents the heartiest co-operation and good will. The wise superintendent will seek advice from his principals on many points, even in selecting and assigning teachers to their respective departments. The principals, in their turn, will do well to freely advise with the teachers. Supervision should not be so strict that it robs the school of individual initiative. Just now there is a demand on the part of teachers for more voice in shaping and administering the policies of the school. These advocates say the present system is autocratic rather than democratic. No doubt this new movement, if not carried too far, will bring about a better organization than we now have. Changes must be wrought carefully, however. Co-operation of teachers in shaping the policies of a school is legitimate, but a strong administration demands, as in national government, one strong administrative head.

A Question of Relationships. The relationship between the Superintendent of a school and the "Board of Education" is not generally understood. Legal statutes, while providing for the position of a superintendent of schools, do not outline his powers and duties to such an extent as they do those of the teacher or the "Board". Different states, cities and teachers' organizations have appointed committees to define the duties and powers of the superintendent. Brief statements from a few of these are here inserted:

"At the head of the school department is the superintendent of schools. His chief function will be the supervision of instruction, but with final jurisdiction subject only to the board of school directors, in the case of other matters than instruction. He should be made the real head and leader of the school system in fact as well as in name, and full responsibility for the successful conduct of all departments of the educational service should be placed squarely on his shoulders. As long as the board has confidence in the judgment and ability of the superintendent, he should be supported in his acts; when they cease to have such confidence, they should call for his resignation. They should not assume authority on educational matters themselves, nor permit him to evade his proper responsibility by putting it off on them. Book agents, applicants for teachers' positions, disgruntled teachers and principals, and persons seeking favors in the educational branch of the school department should at once be referred to the superintendent of schools, with the statement that the board makes it a rule to take no action except upon his recommendation."—**The Portland, Oregon, Survey.**

"The proper lines of demarcation between the functions of a school board and a superintendent are perfectly clear. The relations should be exactly similar to those between the board of directors of a railway or manufacturing or banking corporation and the active managers of those concerns. The directors advise and recommend, and, if need be, check the president in too rapid expansion of the business or in a manifestly unwise policy. But the successful corporation is managed by a generally unhampered and well-supported president, whose reputation is at stake and whose interests are bound up with those of the stockholders. The same must be true of a school system. The superintendent should be very carefully and wisely chosen, and then held fully responsible for the success of the schools. Just as the president of a railroad must be free to select his expert assistants, so must the superintendent be free to select his teachers, even his janitors. When he proves unable to do this wisely he has proved his unfitness for his position."—Report of a Survey of the Public School of Leavenworth, Kans.

"The individual board member should not attempt to dictate school policies to the superintendent or to listen to complaints from principals, teachers or parents. All such complaints should be referred to the superintendent. An individual board member does not have the authority of even the lowest paid employe, unless the board by resolution has delegated him to exercise authority in certain matters. A board of education should employ a superintendent of schools to act as its executive officer. To him it should delegate the authority to nominate teachers, to recommend their dismissal, to select text-books, to formulate courses of study, to recommend increases in teachers' salaries for efficient service, and to have general supervision of instruction."—Survey Report, Ogden, Utah.

"The superintendent occupies a position of peculiar responsibility. He is the intermediary between the public and the schools. His function resembles that of the architect as an intermediary between owner and contractor. He must verify the validity of the demands of the community. He must then reconcile the demands with educational possibilities. He must take all the suggestions given by the community and then embody them in a workable educational program. This the community cannot do; neither can it be done by the board. Just as an architect in the case of a building, they lack the special qualifications for the expert adjustment of the details. Community and board can tell what they want; then under their supervision the superintendent will draw up the courses of study, select the text-books to be used, select the supplementary books, apparatus, equipment, select teachers who have the necessary qualifications for doing the work desired, etc. It is he who is in a position best to understand these various technical educational matters. The responsibility for the labors should necessarily be placed upon his shoulders, with those less expert sitting in supervisory capacity. In thus placing responsibility upon the superintendent the board is not thereby relieved. They must approve or disapprove of the results of his labors. In order to judge wisely, they must be in contact with the schools. They must know his actual labors, not his mere statement of them. They should visit the schools, observe, discuss, and lead in community discussion. Unless they know rather intimately the way their suggestions work out in actual educational practice, they are not in a position to approve or disapprove of the decisions of the superintendent. School board members are not supposed to be mere rubber stamps. They must know what is going on."— **Survey Report, San Antonio, Texas.**

"They (the school board) should not make the common mistake of attempting to assume authority on educational matters themselves, concerning which they cannot act intelligently, nor should they permit the superintendent of schools to evade his proper responsibility by putting it off on them.

"This does not mean that the board of school trustees will have nothing left to do. On the contrary, there will still be plenty left for them to manage. It simply means that in those matters which are matters of expert judgment, and which no board of laymen is competent to decide, they ought to act only on the recommendation of the educational expert they employ, and ought to trust. It is a sheer waste of public funds to pay $4,000 for an educational expert, and then disregard his advice and judgment.

"In all matters such as the hygienic aspects of schoolhouse construction, the authorizing of courses of study, the selection of text and supplemental books, passing on the competency of instruction or the efficiency of the service in the school department,—matters which no board of laymen is competent to pass intelligently upon, —action should be based only on the recommendation of the expert educational office of the board.

"This leaves the board free to attend to the main business which they are elected to handle, and frees them from the hundreds of petty annoyances incident to the personal pulls and influences which beset any lay school board which attempts to exercise expert functions."— School Survey Report, Butte, Montana.

CHAPTER III

Employment and Assignment of Teachers and Other Employes

Comparative Importance. Perhaps the most important task the Board of Education has to perform is to employ superintendent, principals and teachers. Some educators estimate that the teacher constitutes 85 per cent of the efficiency of a school. From the educational standpoint the teacher is at least a vital factor in the school. With the average Board of Education, also, this duty is the one it is least capable of performing. This is no criticism either on the intelligence or the general ability of the "Board" members.

The average "Board" member knows considerable regarding laying out of grounds, construction of buildings, purchase of equipment, supplies, etc. His practical experience and business ability has brought him in contact with such matters. He also knows how to estimate costs, figure levies, etc. Teaching is a special profession, however, which the average "Board" member can not be expected to understand. He does not know the elements which enter into the training of a teacher for service. He cannot understand the kind of training nor the type of personality of the teacher which counts for success in leadership of school children, for he can not get the teacher's point of view. Only one trained in the psychology of childhood and in the profession of teaching can make a careful estimate of a teacher's ability to succeed with pupils, and such a one sometimes errs in judgment.

Employing a Superintendent. In employment of those to be instructors in the school, the first and most important duty is the selection of a superintendent. This is too important a matter to be left with a committee, either to choose or to recommend. The whole "Board" should consider this matter together and discuss the candidates freely. The author knew one "Board" member with seventeen years' experience as a member and twelve of these years as president of the "Board", who, in choosing a superintendent, took the various candidates as they appeared, and introduced them to several business men, citizens and patrons of the school. He did this so that it was informal and seemingly incidental. When the candidate had left the community, this president of the "Board" would casually drop in on those to whom he had introduced him, and without arousing suspicion of his motive, ascertain how the candidate had impressed his new acquaintances. In this way he was able to determine, to some extent, the bearing the candidate's personality had on others.

The usual plan of advertising a vacancy in the office of superintendent of the school and then waiting until from a score to a hundred candidates have applied, many of them in person, is doubtful in both justice and efficiency. But one candidate can be employed, yet many go to much expense in traveling to make personal application. A better method is to seek out quietly several available persons and investigate their record. These may, if desired, be asked to make personal application. The "Board" should, in fairness, reimburse such candidates for the expense of the visit. If the candidate spends two or three days in making the visit, which is of intended benefit to the two parties, the "Board" visited should, as its share, bear the expense of the trip. It would seem that no superintendent ought to be employed until at least a majority of the board members have met him personally. This ought not to be an "unsight and unseen" transaction.

Another method is for the Board of Education to ask the state educational officials or some other experienced and prominent educators to recommend two or three suitable persons for the local superintendency. A committee of the "Board" can then visit the districts where such recommended persons are serving and investigate their work in such community.

It is better that a person chosen for superintendent should have had experience as superintendent in another school, or have had supervision work of some nature. Training in school supervision and administration while in college or normal school is a substitute of some value if actual experience has not been secured. It is needless to say that superintendents should have had teaching experience.

It is usually considered that a superintendent should have scholastic training equal to or greater than the teachers who are to teach with him, as he is to be their educational leader. In a large school system, however, it often occurs that a special teacher in some department has a higher "degree" than the superintendent. The teachers' training has been special, while the superintendent's training has been general. The work of the latter is that of an organizer and an administrator rather than a teacher. His experience has probably been broader and more extended and he may be highly successful in his work. It need not disqualify him, therefore, if one or more of his teachers rank higher in college or university recognition.

The matter of age is a matter to consider in selecting a superintendent. All agree that he should be neither too young a man nor too old, yet the question is, "How young or how old may he be?" No definite rule can be given. One superintendent may be mature at twenty-four and another a boy at thirty. Again, one superintendent may be old and out of touch with young life at forty, while another may be young and ambitious at sixty-five. One of the best and most enthusiastic superintendents the writer knows is seventy years of age. He gets excellent results and is a favorite with students. In a small school system it is more important that the superintendent be young in spirit and in outlook, for the reason that he comes in more direct touch with the student body. At the same time he should have maturity of judgment. In a large school system, where the superintendent does not come so much in direct contact with students, but reaches them through principals and teachers and his problems are larger and more complex, there seems to be no valid reason why the superintendent should lose value at fifty or fifty-five years of age any more than in other professions or occupations. Business and government work attest to the fact that the heavier burdens and responsibilities are borne successfully by men and women from fifty to seventy years of age. Experience in supervision and administration should be a strong factor for consideration in employment of a superintendent. An inexperienced superintendent, unless he be especially trained for supervisory and administrative work in education, is likely to pass through several experimental years before he becomes proficient; he is apt, indeed, to do the school system more harm than good.

One other phase ought to be mentioned, and that is the source from which superintendents may legitimately be drawn. As mentioned in the preceding paragraph, they should be persons with teaching experience. A normal school graduate or a college graduate may assume the superintendency of a school directly without teaching experience and perhaps in time become successful. If so, he does it by gradually experimenting and by learning from his kindly tolerant teachers. The chances are against his being a valuable superintendent for several years. It is a decided mistake to employ such in this capacity.

A superintendent of a small school is gaining experience which naturally fits him for the superintendency in a larger system, and this is the source from which most of the superintendents in the better schools are drawn. Occasionally it happens that a high school principal is promoted to the superintendency of the school. If he has previously supervised grades or taught in the grades this may be a wise choice, but if not, such a choice is experimental. Such a superintendent is apt to give too much attention to the high school end of the work, where he is familiar, and at best it will be a long time before he understands grade problems. A more logical source, it would seem, would be the selection of a ward principal for the superintendency, if he meets qualifications educationally. The selection of a county superintendent as head of a school system is seldom followed, although in many ways a county superintendent's experience would be a valuable asset in such a position. The county superintendent is now divorced from politics in many states, so this need be no objection.

The question may arise as to whether a man or a woman should be chosen to be the head of a school system. Thus far a preponderance of superintendents have been men. There seems to be no objection "a priori" why a woman may not be selected, and cases may be mentioned where women have been selected and have made records as successful school administrators and supervisors. However, the usual choice of a man for such position may be justified on two grounds. First, the rank and file of teachers, especially in the grades, are women. In the Primary and Intermediate grades women are better adapted to the work than are men. To balance the matter and to bring pupils in their educational experience into contact with both feminine and masculine natures it is only reasonable to employ some men as instructors and administrators in the upper departments of the school. In the smaller schools it often occurs that the superintendent is the only male member of the faculty. In such case the employment of a woman as superintendent would leave the school one-sided in this respect. There is no doubt that such a situation would lessen the appeal of the school to the larger boys, at least. The superintendent represents the school in the community and comes into contact with the Board members and business men. This is the second obvious reason why Boards of Education usually prefer a man for superintendent of the school. It is no reflection on the ability of women.

Selection of Principals. What has been said regarding the selection of a superintendent applies also in large measure to selection of principals. Several differences exist, however. The Board of Education here has the assistance of a superintendent in making a choice. The position of a principal, also, is more specific in its nature and therefore less general, especially as regards the high school. Not so much administrative ability is needed, but the principal should be a good instructor and a strong supervisor. A ward principal may be chosen from among the superintendents of smaller school systems or may come from the ranks of the teacher. If he teaches, it is usually better that he instruct in the higher grades of the building, as he will thus better command the respect of the entire body of pupils. Many schools employ lady ward principals, and with excellent results. A high school principal also may be chosen from the ranks of superintendents of smaller school systems, and should be one with a strong bent for high school work. It is, of course, better if the high school principal has had experience as a high school instructor.

Selection and Assignment of Teachers. The selection of teachers is perhaps most important because there are comparatively more of them, and because they touch most closely the life of the pupils. Personality here is a vital factor, and personality is difficult to judge. A superintendent should use great care in his recommendation of teachers, and the Board of Education should then respect the superintendent's judgment and accept his recommendations, unless exceptionally strong reasons exist why the recommendations should not be accepted. The preparation and experience of teacher candidates should be known, and when possible the superintendent should have a personal interview with applicants. It is still better if he is able to see each teacher applicant at work in another school and to ascertain the measure of her worth there. A Board of Education may well afford to expend a reasonable amount in traveling expenses of a superintendent in investigating the work of prospective teachers, and many Boards of Education are accustomed to do so.

The qualities of a candidate to be considered are, educational preparation, professional training, teaching experience, moral character and personality. It is not always necessary, of course, that a teacher should have had actual experience in a school on her own responsibility, in order to be favorably considered for a position. A good substitute for actual experience is practice teaching in a suitable training school. Indeed, it may not always be that an experienced teacher is superior to an inexperienced teacher. This all depends on the kind of experience. Some types of experience are worse than none at all. In considering both training and experience it is well to inquire whether such pertains to the position to be filled. Evidently an applicant with Primary training but no experience is better adapted to a Primary position than an experienced Grammar school teacher without Primary training.

In the past, too little attention has been given to the matter of proper education and training of teachers. There has been somehow a general feeling that if a teacher has had experience she should be a good teacher. Educators are now coming to see that experience is but one factor, and not the stronger factor. Scholastic preparation, study of methods and proper training are also necessary. In brief, it is felt that a high school teacher should be a college graduate with a degree, and that her course in college should include strong work in Education. A grade teacher should be a two-year Normal School graduate and have had considerable training in teaching. A special supervisor should meet the same demands and have majored in her special subject. A principal or superintendent should be a college graduate with a degree, his course to include much in Education, and he also should, if possible, have taken a course in School Administration and Supervision. No superintendent should be employed as such who has not had experience in teaching, and it is better if he has also had experience in administration and supervision.

The question may be asked, "Where may a superintendent find suitable teachers, in a normal school, college, university, or through an agency?" The answer is, "In all these." Reputable schools are usually a safe source. Some states provide free placement bureaus for such purposes. Commercial agencies of good standing are also to be trusted. Another source is to find them in service in other schools. This, of course, is intended to mean when employing teachers for a succeeding year, a term beyond the contract period the teacher is then serving. It is both unethical and non-professional to induce a teacher to break a contract. Teachers are practically always employed by the school year, from September to June, in the graded and high schools, so it is perfectly legitimate for a school to secure a teacher from another school for the following year.

Another question sometimes arises concerning the employment of teachers. Is it better to employ resident teachers or non-resident teachers? There are certain advantages in each plan. The resident teacher is better known by the local school authorities as to character, personality, etc. She is apt, also, to have more interest in the community, and may be a more valuable asset in this way. She knows the local situation better; knows the possibilities and limitations of the school. If the community is small she knows the personnel of her pupils, the home conditions, etc. On the other hand, she herself has handicaps in the same way. Both the pupils and parents know the peculiarities and limitations of the teacher. She is thus open to freer criticism. Especially if the teacher is young and inexperienced, will this be true. If she is a teacher then in the high school department, there is a tendency for her to be called by her given name by the students. Such familiarity is usually detrimental to the teacher's control and influence. It takes more courage to get rid of a mediocre teacher if she is a resident of the community. The employment of a non-resident teacher avoids, of course, these things. However, she is more apt to lack interest in community affairs. She is also prone to go from school to school on inducement of a slightly larger salary. If all teachers are non-resident it makes for serious lack of permanency in the school; if all home teachers are employed it tends to narrowness in policy and method. The "happy medium" is better, where there are both some home teachers and some non-resident teachers employed in each building and each department. In employment of home teachers some boards of education require that the teacher shall first have had successful experience in some other school. This would seem to be a wise provision.

In employment of teachers none should be employed for family nor for political reasons, nor because the teacher needs a job. The school should be placed neither on a political nor a charitable basis. Any board member who lends his vote to such a practice is either too incompetent or too weak to represent his district in an official capacity. The good of the children is more to be considered than the good of any teacher or any teacher's family.

A matter too little considered in many schools is the proper assignment of teachers. A teacher's contract usually assigns her to teach in a certain grade and perhaps in a certain building, or to teach certain subjects. The applicant often applies for a position, not because she is particularly adapted to it, but because that is the position she knows to be vacant. She may fit better in another position than the one to which her contract assigns her. A few "Boards" use more freedom, by designating in the contract that the teacher is to teach in the Primary Department, the Intermediate Department, etc. This plan enables the superintendent to place her in a room or on a subject where she is most needed, or may even permit her transfer if necessary. Some unsuccessful teachers may become successful when thus transferred to another room or given other subjects to teach.

One prominent educator of the United States advocates promoting a teacher year by year with her class, to avoid the pupils having frequent change of teachers.

He would have a teacher begin with the First Primary grade and keep the same class until it completes the Eighth grade. This is no doubt extremely radical, as no teacher can be expected to be especially trained for so wide a field of service. The idea might be practical over a narrower range, however. There seems to be no valid reason why a teacher trained for Primary work might not take a class through the three Primary grades, an Intermediate teacher through the three Intermediate grades, or a Grammar School teacher through the two Grammar School grades. This would give pupils the same teacher for two or three years.

The work of the High School is usually specialized, one teacher instructing in English, another in Science, etc. This gives each teacher some work with each grade of the High School, but this plan of course tends to narrowness and lack of correlation. Some superintendents, while assigning each teacher most of her work along her special line, assign her one or two other subjects, to give the teacher the wider view of the school work and better to keep in operation the correlation feature. One prominent educator advocates that each High School teacher be given one class in English, so that this subject will be better correlated with all other work.

There is another point in the assignment of teachers not sufficiently considered. In this department there are several groups of related subjects, such as English, Science, etc. While all these groups need well prepared teachers, some need more maturity of judgment and experience in life's school to interpret most efficiently. The English and Social Science fields ought to have teachers of experience and mature judgment, if the students are to receive the best interpretation of life's problems and the most inspiration in the class-room. Yet how often we find the younger teachers assigned to the

English and the Social Science subjects. Somehow there is a feeling among superintendents and school officials that any instructor can teach English or History, but the demand is for a special teacher for Science, Mathematics or Foreign Language. There is at least room for serious consideration at this point.

The Special Teacher, or Supervisor.   In the past few years there has developed in the larger schools a new class of teachers known as the special teacher, or supervisor of a special subject or subjects.   Teachers in various schools have been chosen to have charge of such special subjects as Vocal Music, Drawing, Penmanship, Physical Culture, Home Economics, and Manual Training.   Inexperienced superintendents are sometimes puzzled to judge the relationship of this type of teacher to the superintendent and to the general teaching force.   Indeed, even the experienced superintendent sometimes finds difficulty in properly "cataloguing" her and keeping her rightly classified.   The supervisor may take herself too seriously, and the teachers in general may be jealous of the special teacher, who seems to "usurp" some of their own authority.

Shall this special teacher teach, supervise, or do both? No doubt in the large city system of schools she should supervise only, or supervise and train the regular teachers to do the work of teaching and training the pupils in the special subject.   In the smaller system, however, there is no reason why such teacher should not teach some in each room and thus bring the inspiration of her special ability directly to the pupils.   If the school system is small enough she may even be able to do all the teaching necessary in her special subject.

Another question arises as to who shall be responsible for the deportment of pupils in a room while the teacher is training pupils. If pupils are taken to a special room for the exercise it would seem that the special teacher should have full charge. On the other hand, if the exercise is conducted in the regular class room the class room teacher should retain her authority and assist in conducting the work, so far as discipline and the attention of pupils to the task is concerned. In any event, if the regular teacher must teach the subject on days when the special teacher is not present in the room, she should be present when the supervisor is conducting the work and give her undivided attention to the class exercise.

The question of authority also may arise. There should, of course, be co-operation, but no special teacher should be allowed to usurp authority in the domain of a regular teacher in her class room. Again, shall the supervisor have authority to call meetings of the teachers for instruction and training? If such meetings be called, they should be called by the superintendent rather than by the supervisor. Shall special teachers be called upon to do hall duty and other general duties? If needed for this purpose, "yes". They are employes of the district and should serve the same as other teachers in special ways. In general, there should be caution that the special teacher and her work be not isolated from the regular school work.

The Choice and Function of a Janitor. So far as the small school is concerned there is often no such thing as "choice" of a janitor, for the "Board" has no choice in the matter but to take whom it can get. In such case the employe is usually an old man who is unable to hold any other position. If he has still good eyesight to see the dust on the furniture, and if he is not too childish to get along with teachers and pupils, the district is fortunate. However, this is the extreme case. Usually, if a just wage is offered and some discernment used on the part of the "Board", a fairly good candidate may be selected.

What characteristics should a candidate have to entitle him to the position of janitor of a school? Evidently a main qualification is ordinary intelligence. Given this and age between twenty-one and sixty, with good physique, the candidate is worth consideration. He should, of course, be of good moral character and be trustworthy. He should not indulge in grossly bad habits and should refrain from bad language about the building. If he is a non-user of tobacco all the better, although this habit need not disqualify a candidate. He should not, at least, indulge in this or any other bad habit in the presence of the pupils. In addition, he should be reasonably adapted to getting along with children. If he has mechanical ability and ingenuity it will be an advantage.

The janitor, although different in his position in the school from the teachers, should be under direction of the superintendent in his regular duties about the school building. Extra duties, such as repair work, may better be under direction of the chairman of the Committee on Buildings and Grounds. It is better that teachers do not attempt the direction of the janitor, but refer such matters to the superintendent or to the principal of the building.

Shall the janitor assume authority over pupils about the building, or be required to assume disciplinary powers at all? Usually it is better if the janitor is freed from all such authority and responsibility. He should, however, be allowed authority before and after school, when the teachers are not present. Many schools require the janitor to remain at the building as a disciplinary measure while teachers are home for lunch. In such case he should have full authority over pupils except the authority to punish. This should never be granted a janitor, but he should report to the principal or the superintendent all violations of the rules of the school, or offences in the matter of discipline. All duties of the janitor, aside from his regular duties in taking care of the building and grounds, should be clearly understood in advance and stated in the contract.

What are the regular duties of a janitor? In general terms they consist of care of buildings and grounds, such as shoveling snow from walks or mowing the campus, heating the buildings, sweeping, dusting, etc. He should take personal charge of the temperature of each room and should inspect the rooms occasionally each day to see that the heating and ventilating are effective. The rooms should be swept each evening and dusted each morning, including desks, furniture and woodwork. Each Friday evening, and more often if necessary, the blackboards should be thoroughly cleaned, as also should the erasers. Chalk trays should be cleaned each evening. Boards may be cleaned by means of a large, heavy woolen dry cloth or a cloth slightly dampened. It is not good for some blackboards to wash them with water or with an oiled cloth.

Once per month or oftener floors should be scrubbed, unless the floors are well oiled. In that case a thorough wiping occasionally with a slightly dampened mop will suffice. All parts of the building should be kept neat and tidy. Ordinary adjustments or slight repairs should be the work of the janitor. Cupboards and other storage places should be kept tidy. Often debris is allowed to collect in recesses about the building, and especially under stairways. Besides giving the building a slovenly appearance this makes an especially dangerous fire hazard.

In general, the janitor has the custody of buildings at all times, both out of and in school hours. He should be furnished with keys to all rooms and should see that the building is properly closed, doors locked and windows fastened each night before leaving the grounds. He may be expected to open and close the buildings for evening use occasionally, although if such calls be frequent justice would dictate that he receive extra compensation for this work. It is usually better that only the janitor, the principal and the superintendent have keys to the building. Responsibility should not be too much scattered.

Some "Boards" employ a janitor for part time or for full time to care for the buildings during the summer vacation, and to make needed repairs. This is both commendable and an economy. It is much less expensive to repair buildings each year, repaint, redecorate, etc., than to neglect such for several years. Flower plots may thus be kept up, the lawn regularly trimmed, playgrounds and gymnasiums rendered usable the year 'round.

CHAPTER IV

Material Equipment

Next to the importance of the teacher as a factor in education is sufficient and proper equipment. In the broad sense this includes grounds and buildings as well as library, apparatus, etc. Of course, these usually are out of control of both superintendent and Board of Education, but they are discussed here for the reason that in building and in remodeling they are largely controllable.

The School Site. The selection of a site for a school is important, and the following matters should be considered:

1. A fairly level or slightly rolling ground, but not a low or swampy ground.

2. Convenient to the center of school population or district, so as to equalize distance for pupils. This is especially important where smaller children attend.

3. Location not to be too near noisy thoroughfare nor railway stations, etc. It is also better if the site is not on a street much used for traffic.

4. A site that will render the building usuable for social center purposes. In the past, school sites have been chosen a considerable distance from the business district, but as the building is now used for so many social purposes and in the evening as well, it is better if it be near the center of the district.

Grounds. The ordinary school ground is much too small for recreation purposes. The newer schools being built, such as the rural consolidated schools, provide more space, usually about five acres. Some of this is intended for agriculture plot rather than for recreation. Some city schools are now requiring for playground purposes a whole block for each building.

For grade pupils, where games requiring large grounds are not played, it is considered that thirty square feet of ground space per pupil is sufficient. This, of course, should be exclusive of grounds used for walks, flower beds, etc. This would approximate nine pupils per square rod of space, or eleven square rods for one hundred pupils. It must be remembered that this should be the minimum. No definite rule can be given as to how much outside space should be provided, as the space depends upon the enrollment, the size and nature of pupils, and the kind of games to be played. A high school needs larger grounds per enrollment than the grades, because of the type of games needing more space.

A visit to many schools will find a dearth of playground equipment. On some school grounds no attempt has been made to provide equipment for play or games. Where such equipment is found it is often of such nature that it can be used by the high school and grammar school pupils only. The needs of the smaller pupils are thus ignored, yet the need for play apparatus for smaller pupils is more apparent than for the larger ones. Some schools are now providing simple equipment, such as sand-piles, swings, teeter-boards, turning-poles, and even slides and giant strides. Most of these are simple and inexpensive and may be made by the janitor, or even be made by the boys in the Manual Training shop. Ropes, poles, planks, gas pipe and ingenuity are all that are necessary to accomplish this. Some commercial firms are now providing excellent playground equipment, and at reasonable price.

Buildings. In the construction of buildings the tendency at present is to make them utilitarian rather than ornamental. The buildings, both on the exterior and in the interior, are simple. The square or the rectangular buildings are the prevailing type, while the flat roof usually obtains. The buildings are ordinarily two stories high above the basement room. The basement room is used for furnace room, gymnasium and vocational shops. In a combination building the elementary grades occupy the main floor, while the upper floor is given over to the high school.

The better types of building now being constructed are fire-proof or semi-fire-proof, and contain lavatories, sanitary flush toilets, and drinking fountains with some form of bubbler. Cloakrooms are of course provided, and in some buildings individual steel lockers are installed, especially for high school and grammar school students. While corridors are convenient, some schools save expense in construction by having small landings only and using all other space for rooms. There should always be separate cloakrooms or corridor space for lockers, as it is most unsanitary to allow wraps to hang in a classroom where pupils are seated. Where possible there should be separate cloakrooms for boys and girls, especially in the upper grades and the high school.

For class rooms, light should enter from above or from one side of the room only, and window space should, in general, be one-fifth the floor space of the room. The windows should extend upward as near the ceiling as possible. Light colored window shades are preferred. Each classroom should contain fifteen square feet of floor space per pupil and two hundred cubic feet of air space per pupil. The height of the room ranges from twelve feet to fourteen feet. No grade room, it is considered, should enroll more than forty pupils, although some consider it wise for each room to have a capacity of forty-eight pupils, to meet emergencies which may occur. The ideal number in a grade room for one teacher is twenty-four to thirty-six pupils. In constructing a building the dimensions of classrooms should correspond to maximum number of pupils to be accommodated. In his book, "School Architecture," Mr. George Bruce gives as suggestive sizes of class rooms:

24x28 feet, 6 rows of six each, 36 pupils.
22x32 feet, 8 rows of five each, 40 pupils.
24x32 feet, 8 rows of six each, 48 pupils.

In each classroom and each recitation room there should be ample blackboard space; in recitation room for all pupils in the class to work at once is ideal, while in grade rooms space for one-half the pupils, or one section, is sufficient. It is usually not desirable to place a blackboard in the rear of the room. In Primary and Intermediate rooms the blackboard should be placed twenty-six to twenty-eight inches from the floor, while in Grammar room and High School room from twenty-eight to thirty-two inches. The usual width of blackboard is four feet, but in Primary and Intermediate rooms forty to forty-four inches is sufficient. Many schools place above the blackboard in these rooms an eighteen-inch strip of burlap for convenience of the teacher in displaying regular and special work. Three types of blackboard are used, natural slate, liquid slating or paint on the plastering, and the woodpulp board.

Most modern school buildings are provided with a gymnasium. This is deemed necessary because much of the school year weather conditions prevent games and exercises on the school ground. The gymnasium usually occupies basement space. The gymnasium, to be suitable for various inside games, should be in dimensions as follows: Length, 66 to 70 feet; width, 30 to 40 feet, and height 16 to 18 feet. It is desirable to provide suitable space for spectators, also. The gymnasium should be made available at different periods in the week to different groups of pupils and not used simply for team-work for a small group of students. It may well be used in the evening for community recreation.

In every school building constructed some provision should be made for an auditorium. This may be used by the school for rehearsals, for school programs, etc. The auditorium is also a valuable asset to the community for neighborhood or community meetings of various kinds. If a separate auditorium cannot be provided, the high school assembly may be so arranged as to answer this need, or the gymnasium may be used. In either case a stage or suitable rostrum should be a feature of the auditorium, and suitable seating be provided.

Every school employing four or more teachers should have a small room, suitably located, to be used as an office. This should be provided with an office desk, a filing case, several chairs and a safe or fire-proof vault for keeping of records and other important papers. The office is necessary for the superintendent, as it provides a place for him in which to hold conferences with pupils, teachers and parents. A rest room, or emergency room, is also desirable, where sick pupils or teachers may be accommodated.

Methods of Heating. The method of heating should receive serious consideration in the construction of a school plant. Aside from the system of heating, the adequacy of the heating plant is important. Some schools have installed plants too small to do the work without crowding the furnace. It is usually considered by janitors that a heating plant barely large enough to heat a building will, by consequent necessary crowding, consume more fuel and with less satisfactory results than a heating plant a size too large. The methods of heating a school building are stove, hot-air furnace, steam, vapor and hot-water. The stove is not advisable except in one-room buildings, and when used should always be surrounded by a jacket. The hot-air furnace is used in but few buildings and is usually unsatisfactory. In a small building the results are better than in a large building. Steam is the prevailing method of heating school buildings and is usually found satisfactory. To be most effective, this system should provide small return pipes from the radiator to the boiler. When the fan system of ventilation is used this is a strong aid to the heating of schoolrooms and in moderate weather is sufficient for heating alone The principle of this is to force into each room air previously warmed by passing over hot coils.

Methods of Ventilation. The most simple method of ventilation is by open windows and open doors. In mild weather this method is also probably the best one. In severe weather it is fraught with much danger to the health of pupils and teacher. Where it must be used, some simple devices are an aid. One or more windows may be lowered a few inches from the top. If a canvas strip eight inches wide be tacked to the top of the window sash and to the top of the window casing the upper sash may safely be dropped eight inches. When it is so dropped the canvas becomes stretched across the opening and prevents direct draft from the wind. A board six inches in width may be fitted under the lower sash, in order to allow some fresh air to enter the room at the middle of the window between the sashes. Again, a small frame across which is stretched canvas or cheesecloth may be inserted under the lower sash.

The gravity system is quite effective and this means of ventilation is often used. Fresh air from out of doors is admitted in the upper part of the inner wall by means of a duct. The air is often first warmed by passing over heated coils. The success of this method depends upon the outlet of the impure air through another duct, so as to complete the circulation. An exhaust duct begins in an opening in the floor or near the lower part of the inner wall of each room and extends upward through the roof of the building. If this duct leads upward close beside the furnace chimney the circulation is increased by heating the exhaust air. Sometimes this exhaust chamber contains a small radiator heated by steam from the boiler, a plan which is still more effective. The fan system described in another paragraph, while the most expensive to install, is usually considered by far the best system of ventilation for school buildings. There is now on the market a unit system of ventilation for each room similar in operation to the fan system, but this has not as yet come into extensive use. In the matter of ventilation two things should be kept in mind, namely, that each pupil in the room is entitled to 200 cubic feet of air space, and that this air should be changed at the rate of a complete change of air in the room every eight minutes. In each grade room or class room, a thermometer should be provided. Remember that for correct registration this should hang on a level with the bodies of pupils when they are seated at their desks. The thermometer should register from sixty-eight to seventy degrees Fahrenheit.

Shops and Laboratories. The modern school requires facilities for vocational work and for experimental work in Science. When such work can have separate rooms it is better. The Manual Training room usually occupies space in the basement. The room should be well lighted and sufficiently heated, and should contain a proper number of benches for the pupils to be accommodated. Regular commercial Manual Training benches, single or double, and containing drawers, are better, although a regular carpenter's workbench may be used. There should be a chest, a case or a cage in which the tools may be kept locked. These should be in charge of the instructor and kept under lock when not in use. The janitor should not have access to these tools for work about the building but should be provided with separate tools for such work. There should be a general set of tools furnished and also individual tools for each bench, of those tools more often used. A small blackboard may be provided for drawings, outlines, etc. If a separate lumber room is not possible, racks should be provided for lumber in the shop. It is well if a separate staining room be provided.

The Domestic Science kitchen is often located in the basement, although an upper available room is preferable. The room should be light, warm and well ventilated. Although long tables are sometimes used, regular individual Domestic Science tables are to be preferred. These should contain drawers for silverware, etc. A pantry or cupboard should be provided for storing general cooking utensils, and a refrigerator in the room is a convenience. Several plans of heating are used for the cooking classes. Simple oil burners are sometimes used, but gasoline stoves should never be used, on account of the fire hazard. Special gas plants are sometimes installed in the building, and gas plates used. Blow gas is sometimes used instead. Where city gas is available this is generally used. Where the building is electrically wired and day current is available, electric stoves may be used, and these are being installed in many schools. Some few of the schools use a coal or a wood range. Whatever system of heating is used, a burner should be provided for every two girls in the class, besides an adequate number of ovens. For the

Sewing class one or more sewing machines should be provided.

Science laboratories may preferably have separate rooms, but a regular recitation room may be utilized. The room should be especially well lighted and be provided with tables or suitable high benches. If possible there should be running water in the room and gas heat or some other heating device. When necessary, alcohol lamps may be used. In small buildings where room is scarce the Domestic Science room may be utilized for Science work. There should be a separate case for laboratory apparatus, and this should be kept locked when not in use. The Science equipment should be of the best quality and of wide enough range to perform the necessary experiments. Some utensils should be supplied in sufficient quantities so that not more than two students need to work together.

Library. Two classes of books may be included in the library, reading books, or fiction, and reference books. The latter is more important for school purposes, but when there is no local public library available the former is also desirable. When these cannot be procured, however, the school may usually get free use of some traveling library.

The reference library has in the past been deemed necessary only for the High School, but opinion is rapidly favoring also a reference library for the Grammar School, and even for the Intermediate grades. The nature of books chosen would, of course, be different in different departments. In general we can say that there should be a complete dictionary in each department, and in the high school of fifty pupils there should be two such dictionaries. In the Intermediate department there ought also to be for each room several briefer dictionaries. **For** all these departments it is well if each pupil may have his individual "Student's Dictionary" at his desk. The High School usually has one of the best, modern, comprehensive encyclopedia sets. Where the High School is large, more than one may be necessary. The Grammar School should have a briefer cyclopedia, a good, modern set of from five to twelve volumes. A world atlas should be in both the Grammar School and the High School.

Reference books should be along the line of subjects pursued and plentiful enough not to hamper the work. Only authentic reference books are worth procuring. All books and book shelves should be properly labeled and a classified list of the books kept. It is well if a reasonable fund is available to superintendent and teachers each year for purchase of new and necessary books. All library books should, of course, be kept in a suitable case or cupboard, and a certain teacher be given charge of the library and held responsible for its proper care.

In choosing reference books it is usually better not to expend funds for extensive sets along certain lines, such as a twenty volume set in History, a twenty-five volume set in Literature, or complete sets of works of an author. The authorship of these are apt to be unsatisfactory, and it is usual that in such purchase only a few volumes of the set will ever be needed or used by the school. Single volumes or small sets are of more service to schools. This, of course, does not apply to the purchase of a general encyclopedia.

Other Equipment. Certain other equipment is necessary in every well organized school. There should be a set of Political Geography maps for each building, so arranged that they may readily be removed to any room. A world globe from twelve to eighteen inches in diameter should be in every building. If this is a globe suspended from the ceiling, extra cords and pulleys may be supplied to the various rooms so that the globe can be easily taken from one room to another. A chart to illustrate Physiology and Hygiene should be provided, and sets of History maps or charts for each department of History taught. Many schools provide also a Nature Study chart and an Agriculture chart. Reading and Phonic charts are necessary for the Primary room and a sand table is valuable. Some schools provide relief maps. Visual instruction is coming to have a place in the better class of schools and constitutes a distinct aid in school work. This takes three forms, the stereoscope and stereographs, the lantern and slides, and the moving-picture machine and the film. Some musical instrument ought to be provided in each building and it is, of course, better to have an instrument in each room. The piano is usually considered better for all departments, but the phonograph is more often used in the grades, both for reasons of economy and because it can easily be moved from room to room.

School Furniture. School furniture consists of tables, bookcases, teacher's desk and pupils' desks, besides all other stationary articles. Wall pictures and clocks may be included in the term.

School desks may be classified as adjustable and non-adjustable. The former are made in two styles, the seat and desk separate and the seat and the desk combined. A new desk being introduced is a combined seat and desk which is so constructed that it does not need to be fastened to the floor. The adjustable seats are of course more hygienic, and are rapidly displacing the old type desk. The movable desk mentioned is convenient especially for the Primary room, and for other rooms where floor space is occasionally needed for games, etc.

The flat-top desk for teachers is preferable, and it should contain plenty of drawers with lock and key. For the superintendent's office a roller-top desk is more convenient. A file case should also be provided in the office. Each classroom should contain a chair with arm supports for the teacher's use, and several chairs for visitors. Where space is meager, folding chairs are a convenience. There should be several chairs in the office.

It is well to have a good-sized clock in each room, so placed that pupils may readily see it. A few well chosen framed pictures should hang on the wall. These should be of a type to appeal to the age of the pupils in the room, and be the work of standard artists. The pictures should not in general be duplicated in the different rooms although certain pictures, such as those of Washington and Lincoln, may well be duplicated in various rooms. The ideal plan for providing pictures for school rooms is to have them graded so that the various departments will have pictures particularly adapted to the interests of children in the department, and at the same time to have the range as a whole extensive enough to be representative of the various subjects and of the works of the leading artists.

There ought to be at least one good enclosed bookcase in each room, and more if necessary. These are better if built into the walls. Glass doors are preferable and sliding doors are better than swinging doors. Bookcases should be provided with lock and key.

Working Material. Besides furnishing general equipment, districts are gradually more and more furnishing working material for pupils. Of course, schools have always furnished blackboard crayons, and usually **exami-**

nation paper. Some schools are now furnishing theme paper and Penmanship practice paper. Some schools also furnish, free to the pupils, pens and ink and Primary lead pencils and drawing pencils. Often Drawing materials are furnished. Construction paper is usually free to Kindergarten and Primary pupils.

It is customary for Manual Training students to pay for lumber and stains used to construct articles for their own use. Girls in the Domestic Science classes usually furnish material for the sewing, while the district furnishes material for the cooking lessons. Sometimes products of cooking lessons are sold to partially reimburse the district for the expense of materials. A few schools charge a laboratory fee to students using the Science laboratory, to pay for chemicals, breakage, etc.

It is usual in most states and districts to require pupils to furnish their own regular texts. A few states, however, require the districts to furnish free texts for use of pupils. In some other states this is optional with each individual district. When the pupils furnish their own texts it is quite general for the district to furnish supplementary reading texts and all other reference books needed. Sets of song books are by many districts furnished for Music work. There seems to be a growing disposition for schools to furnish more working material and pupils to furnish less.

Of course, schools should furnish to teachers the necessary daily registers and other record books for the school. These should include daily class record books, plan books, etc., also desk copies of texts they are required to teach. These are, of course, labeled as property of the school and are not the property of the teachers.

The providing of material of various kinds necessitates proper facilities for storing the material. There should be some organized method, also, of keeping a check on its use. Teachers should be held responsible for the proper distribution and use of materials and for proper care of accessory helps of all kinds. Some schools require teachers and principals to invoice articles and materials both at the beginning and at the close of the school year.

Before closing this chapter a word of caution ought to be given school officials and administrators. When expensive apparatus and material are purchased they should be made available to the pupils and be used as occasion requires. The superintendent should see that each teacher knows what is available in the building, and in supervision should observe whether it is properly utilized. Boards of Education are usually willing to furnish necessary material for the school. When they do so they have a right to expect that it be used. Both superintendent and teachers are sometimes at fault in this matter. It is well for the superintendent to place in the hands of each teacher and each principal a printed list of equipment and material available for use.

A word of warning also may not be out of place in regard to the purchase of equipment for schools. Irresponsible sales agents often solicit school officials for the purchase of articles that appear valuable but that are both unnecessary and impractical in the classroom. In such cases it is well to consult those in a position to know better concerning these matters.

CHAPTER V

Building a Course of Study

Purpose of a Definite Course. It is plain that every well organized school should have a definite course of study, and for the following reasons:

1. That there may be a definite goal for the work of each teacher, and for the school as a whole.

2. That each teacher may know the portion of the work for which she is responsible, and know also the work the other teachers are doing.

3. That the work may be the better correlated.

4. To prevent frequent modifications by teachers who prefer certain subjects or certain phases of the work, and hence might otherwise overstress them.

5. That the work of the school may co-ordinate closely with that of other schools so that pupils transferring from one school to another may continue their work without loss or interruption.

6. So as to make possible a graded system.

Who Is Responsible for the Course of Study. Primarily the Board of Education is responsible for shaping the course, and no course should be made or modified without its being submitted to the "Board" for approval. If the school is a standard school, ranked as such by county or state authorities, the course should be submitted, also, to such authorities for approval.

The framing or modifying of a course of study is actually accomplished, however, by superintendent, principals and teachers. A wise superintendent will always consult principals and teachers, or in a large system representatives from such, when making or changing a course of study. Incidentally it should be noted that frequent changes are detrimental to the work; changes should not be made on whims, but should be backed by logical reasons.

The Course of Study a Tradition. It is often criticised that the course of study is a tradition. This may be, however, a compliment rather than a criticism. The finest things in our civilization are traditional, and things traditional were first backed by good reason and have stood the test of time. This, however, does not argue that we must always cling to old traditions. We may wisely, at times, establish new methods or new systems that in future time may themselves become valuable traditions. Experience in education has proven that each new age places emphasis on different phases of education, on different subject matter and on different methods. No course of study should be unchangeable.

Custom has established as the subject matter for the eight elementary grades the so-called "common branches." These embrace in a general way the fields of English, Mathematics, History, Science and Handwork. Originally the English included but oral Reading, Spelling and Grammar; the Mathematics, Arithmetic; the History, United States History; Science, the study of Geography, and Handwork, Penmanship.

In more recent years the elementary work has expanded to include as follows: English—Reading, oral and silent, Spelling, Language and Grammar; Mathematics—Numbers and Arithmetic; Science—Nature Study, Geography, Hygiene and Physiology; History—Biography, Beginnings of American History in Europe, United States History, and Civics; Vocational work — Penmanship, Manual Training, Domestic Science and Handwork; Art —Music and Drawing.

The High School course is more recent in development. At present it includes the fields of English, Mathematics, Science, Social Science, Vocations, Commerce and Foreign Language. In Normal Training high schools such subjects as Psychology, Pedagogy and Practice Teaching are offered.

English usually includes two years' work of Composition and Rhetoric, one year's work of History of English Literature and one year's work of American Literature, given in this order. Each year some classics are read and some oral English required. Some additional books are also required to be read and reported by each student.

The Mathematics includes a year of Algebra, usually to the subject of Quadratics, a year of Plane Geometry and a half year of Arithmetic, given in this order. Some schools also offer a half year or a year in the subject of Bookkeeping. Certain schools in addition offer as electives a half year in Advanced Algebra and a half year in Solid Geometry. Unified Mathematics are sometimes used either preceding Algebra and Geometry or in lieu of these subjects.

Science usually includes a year of General Science work, a half year or a year of Agriculture, a half year of advanced Physiology and a year of Physics. Some schools also offer a half year in Physiography. In the larger high schools where subjects may be made elective, where a regular Science instructor is employed and where a real Science laboratory may be provided, courses also include a half year in Zoology and a half year in Botany, or a full year in Biology. A few large systems of schools also offer a half year or a year in Chemistry.

The Social Science subjects include a year in Ancient History, a year in Mediaeval and Modern History and a year in American History and American Government, given in this order. The course is now being modified so as to devote a year only to Ancient and Mediaeval History and a full year to Modern History. The tendency at present is to reduce European History to one year, including the fields of Ancient, Mediaeval and Modern History, the emphasis being on the latter. Text-books are now published suitable for this plan. Schools able to offer elective subjects sometimes offer a half year in English History, although a full year offered in Modern History makes this less necessary. A half year in Economics is usually offered, and sometimes a half year in Sociology. Publishers of high school text-books are now offering for consideration an Elementary Social Science text designed for a year's work in the first year of the high school. Many schools also offer a half year in Community Civics in the first year or the second year of the high school.

The vocational subjects include Manual Training for the boys and Home Economics for the girls, usually a year of each. Agriculture is often named as a vocational subject and in some states is, on that basis, legally required.

Regarding the vocational subjects, these are usually confined to the Grammar Department and the High School. Agriculture is considered a high school subject and is given as a credit subject in either the ninth grade or the tenth grade. It is not usual to offer more than one year of the subject, and the real small high school often offers but a half year. Of course, schools large enough to offer several courses may establish a distinct vocational course and offer more work in all these subjects.

Commercial subjects may be included in the term "Vocational", although they are not usually so designated. The subjects included are Bookkeeping, Commercial Arithmetic, Business English, Commercial Law, Penmanship, Shorthand and Typewriting. Commercial courses in large high schools sometimes include the subjects of Salesmanship, Advertising, Journalism, etc.

Foreign Languages now being offered are Latin, French and Spanish. Greek, although a language common in the college, is seldom offered in the high school. More often but two years of a foreign language are offered, although schools able to offer special courses sometimes offer four years of such.

A number of high schools are now offering for credit a semester's work or two semesters' work in Bible Study, given as an elective. Both Vocal Music and Instrumental Music are sometimes offered as credit subjects in the high school, the former as glee club work and the latter as orchestra work. Public Speaking as an elective credit subject is occasionally offered, although this is more often linked up with the last two years of English work.

The Grade Course. Courses of study in the grades vary but little in different schools, except that the Seventh and the Eighth grade work is some different when these grades are included in the Junior High School or when they constitute an Intermediate department in the 6-2-4 plan. In such cases these grades cease to be a part of the elementary department and become a part of the high school department, with consequent changes in type of work.

The Primary Course is simple, usually including the subjects of Reading, Phonics, Handwork, Writing, Story Telling or Oral Language, and Drawing. The Intermediate department is more pretentious and has a more carefully arranged course of study. Real text-book work begins here. A Language text is ordinarily introduced a year previously, however, beginning in the Third grade. The Language series by texts usually includes a three-book series, Book One for grades three and four, Book

Two for grades five and six, and Book Three for grades seven and eight.   The latter text is usually a Grammar text instead of a Language text, or sometimes a combination of the two.   It is customary, also, for a text in Arithmetic to be introduced in the Third grade.   Arithmetics are offered in two-book series or three-book series, the field of work carried in each grade being the same in either case.   The three-book series offers Book One for Grades III and IV.   This text usually stresses the "Four Fundamentals", simple problems, simple Fractions and simple Decimals.   Simple Measurements also are included.   Book Two, designed for Grades V and VI, covers the general field of operations in any Arithmetic, so that pupils compelled to leave school at the close of the sixth year will have some knowledge of the various phases of the subject.   Book Three, for Grades VII and VIII, covers the same field as the previous text, but in a more comprehensive way.   The Seventh grade pursues the text to the subject of simple interest, while the Eighth grade completes the text.

Political Geography succeeds Nature Study in the course and the text-book is usually first used in the Fourth grade.   Previous to this, local Geography and drawing of simple maps may be taught.   Geography texts are usually of a two-book series; Book One, designed for Grades IV and V, and Book Two, designed for Grades VI and VII.   Some schools find it an advantage to use a simple Primary Geography to precede the Elementary Geography, using it in the last half of Grade III or the first half of Grade IV.   Each text of the two-book series covers the whole field of Geography, but the last book in a more comprehensive manner.

A Hygiene text may be introduced in the Fourth grade, although the rule is not universal.   This subject is sometimes given by text twice per day during the fourth year and the fifth year. The Sixth grade may or may not require use of text in Hygiene, but a Physiology text is usually used in Grade VII.

Formal History work by text begins in Grade VI. The first year is devoted to simple United States History, perhaps told biographically. Many schools follow in the Seventh grade with a text on "Beginnings of American History in Europe", or "Background of American History". This permits pupils who must leave school at the close of the Sixth grade to get the field of American History, the most important part. A text in regular American History is usually studied in the eighth year, as is also a text in American Government, for a half year.

Spelling by text is usually scheduled from about the Third grade to the Eighth grade inclusive. Spelling in the previous grades is often in connection with Reading or with Phonics. Sometimes Word Analysis instead of Spelling is given in the Seventh and Eighth grades. Usually Spelling is given daily, although in the Grammar room it is sometimes alternated with Penmanship or some other subject.

Formal Penmanship is conducted in all grades of the Intermediate department and in the Grammar department, and sometimes in the Primary department as well. In the Grammar department the practice period is longer and often alternates with some other subject. Some schools begin formal Penmanship in the Third grade, and some even in the First grade.

Drawing work is given in all grades and often alternates with Penmanship. or with Vocal Music. Music is usually required in all grades. In the upper grades it is given but two or three days per week. General singing is usually conducted in all departments, either in connection with formal Music study, or separately.

While the vocational subjects are stressed more in the high school, Manual Training and Home Economics are often begun in the grades. Here they are given one or two hours per week only, and in the Seventh and Eighth grades. Occasionally these subjects are begun thus as early as the Sixth grade. Grade work in Home Economics consists mostly of sewing by hand, although some schools give some cooking lessons in the Eighth grade. Elementary Agriculture is occasionally taught in the Eighth grade of the school, but it is usually not considered practicable here.

A new subject now being largely included in grade schools is Citizenship Training. In the first six grades this is given a special period two or three days per week, while in the Seventh and Eighth grades it is correlated with United States History and Civics. Ordinarily no text is used by pupils below the Seventh grade.

In outlining a course of study for the grades, the following plan of major subjects and minor subjects may be a convenience. This course is suggestive, and would need to be modified to meet local needs and state requirements. Major subjcts are more important only from the standpoint of requiring more time. Minor subjects may, if necessary, be offered two or three periods per week instead of daily.

I. Primary Department
   Grade 1
   (a) Major subjects.
       Reading (two Primers and two First Readers), Phonics, Oral Language and Story Telling.
   (b) Minor subjects.
       Health Talks and Health Chores, Games, Music, Citizenship Training, Industrial Arts: Hand-

work, Drawing, etc., Nature Study, Number Work (incidental).

Grade 2

(a) Major subjects.

Reading (one First Reader and three Second Readers), Phonics and Spelling, Language and Story Telling, Oral and Written Number Work, with text in hands of teacher.

(b) Minor subjects.

Health Talks and Health Chores, Games, Nature Study, Music, Citizenship Training, Industrial Arts: Handwork, Drawing, etc.

Grade 3

(a) Major subjects.

Reading (four Third Readers), Phonics and Spelling, Language and Story Telling, Elementary Arithmetic, with text, Home Geography one-half year, Biography Stories one-half year. (These may be alternated daily instead, or one subject given thrice per week and the other twice per week.)

(b) Minor subjects.

Hygiene, Music, Citizenship Training, Industrial Arts, Handwork, Drawing, Writing, etc.

II. Intermediate Department

Grade 4

(a) Major subjects.

Reading (three Readers), Spelling and Dictionary Study, Oral Language and Written Composition, Elementary Arithmetic, Elementary Geography, Hygiene one-half year, History Stories of home state, one-half year. (These may alternate daily, instead, or one subject be given thrice per week and the other twice per week.)

(b) Minor subjects.

Music, Citizenship Training, Penmanship, Drawing.

Grade 5

(a) Major subjects.

Reading (three Readers), Spelling and Dictionary Study, Oral Language and Written Composition, Elementary Arithmetic, Elementary Geography, Hygiene one-half year, U. S. History Stories one-half year. (These may be alternated daily, instead, or one subject be given thrice per week and the other twice per week.)

(b) Minor subjects.

Music, Citizenship Training, Penmanship, Drawing.

Grade 6

(a) Major subjects.

Reading (three Readers), Spelling and Dictionary Study, Advanced Arithmetic, Oral Language and Composition, Advanced Geography, Elementary United States History.

(b) Minor subjects.

Music, Citizenship Training, Penmanship, Drawing.

III. Grammar Department

Grade 7

(a) Major subjects.

Reading (two Readers or one Reader and several Classics), Spelling and Word Analysis, Advanced Arithmetic, Composition and Grammar, Advanced Geography, Beginnings of American History in Europe one-half year, Physiology one-half year.

(b) Minor subjects.

Music, Citizenship Training, Penmanship, Drawing, Manual Training and Domestic Science.

Grade 8

(a) Major subjects.

Reading (two Readers or one Reader and several Classics), Spelling and Word Analysis, Advanced Arithmetic, Composition and Grammar, American History, Government in State and Nation.

(b) Minor subjects.

Music, Drawing, Penmanship, Manual Training and Domestic Science.

The High School Course. While the Grade Course of Study is rather rigidly fixed, this is not true to such an extent in the high school. The former includes in subject matter the tools of education, while the latter includes rather the materials of education. Local needs and demands, therefore, may to some extent govern the choice of subjects in the high school. For the small high school, able to offer but one course, this should be a general, and not a special course.

Large high schools may offer two or more courses, some providing as high as six different courses from which the student may select his work. Among the courses provided are: English Course, Foreign Language, or Classical Course, Commercial Course, Normal Training Course and Vocational Course. In general, the differentiation for special courses begins in the Junior year of the High School. The small high school can not advantageously offer special courses or even elective subjects, owing to small number of students and limited number of instructors. It is not generally considered economy, nor really desirable, to offer either elective subjects or special courses unless such subject or course enrolls ten students, certainly not when it enrolls fewer than six students. A smaller number in a class does not offer interest enough to the work, besides requiring an unnecessary number of instructors.

A course of study, and especially a general course, should be well balanced; that is, should include a proper number of subjects and a proportionate amount of time in the several fields of knowledge, such as Science, Mathematics, etc. In addition, the various subjects should be offered in proper sequence. It would be manifestly unwise to offer American History before Modern History, Geometry before Algebra, or Physics before General Science. The course here offered is given as illustrative of the two points mentioned in this paragraph, and not as a model for any school to follow. Balance of subject matter and sequence of subjects are to be kept in mind. Foreign Language is here omitted, but by slight rearrangement, this may be offered in the third and fourth years. In a general course it is not considered best to offer more than two years of Foreign Language, and these should be in the Junior and Senior years, according to opinion of most experienced school authorities.

Suggestive Course of Study Showing Balance of Subject Matter and Proper Sequence of Studies

First Year	Second Year
English (Composition and Rhetoric).	English (Composition and Rhetoric).
Algebra (to Quadratics).	Plane Geometry.
General Science.	Commercial Geography, ½ yr.
Manual Training—for boys.	Agriculture, ½ year.
Domestic Science—for girls.	Ancient and Mediaeval History.

Third Year	Fourth Year
English Literature.	American Literature.
Arithmetic, ½ year.	Physics.
Physiology, ½ year.	American History, ½ year.
Modern History.	American Government, ½ yr.
Economics, ½ year.	Sociology, ½ year.
Commercial Law, ½ year.	Industrial History, ½ year.

It will be observed here that the field of English has four years, Science three years, Social Science four years, Mathematics two and one-half years, and Vocational work one and one-half years. None of these, except the vocational work, is of a special nature. In a general course it is not usually wise to include subjects of a particular nature; for instance, a half year or a year of Bookkeeping is of doubtful value unless a full Commercial Course can be offered, while the offering of Psychology or Pedagogy is likewise unwarranted unless a Normal Training Course is offered.

While local demand may legitimately have its influence in shaping a course of study in the High School, this should come from a real need and not from a whim of a certain group of students. The practice sometimes found of allowing classes each year to vote their choice of two or three subjects is pernicious. When electives are offered they should be offered to individual students rather than to classes, and only in schools large enough for sectioning of classes. A subject should never be offered simply because some instructor is prepared for and desires to teach it; the school is not intended to be a training school for superintendent, principal or teacher, but wholly for the best interest of the students.

The Completed Course. When a course of study is completed it should be arranged in printed or mimeographed form, with copies enough for distribution to all

teachers and school officials.   Except in a large school
system it is not advisable to go to the trouble and expense
of preparing a course of study in pamphlet form of fifty
or one hundred pages.   Such pamphlets are of value for
only two or three years.   A brief circular or folder may
well be printed, or mimeographed copies prepared in sufficient numbers to distribute to students and patrons.
These should contain a synopsis of the course of study,
the texts in use and some general rules of the school.   If
prepared each year, these may also contain the names of
school officials, and the names of teachers and their
departments.

CHAPTER VI

Organization of the School

The proper organization of a school is important, as this renders both administration and supervision more easy. While the general plan of organization into grades and departments is well understood, there are some general considerations which ought to be noted.

Relative Importance of Grades. Among school officials and others there is a tendency to underestimate the relative importance of the grades, or the elementary department of the school. This, perhaps, comes partly from the fact that the organization here is more simple, and in part, from the fact that there are fewer organizations here to claim attention. In comparison to number of pupils involved, however, the elementary school is more important than the high school, as the enrollment is several times as large here as in the high school. No doubt, also, the real bent educationally is more often developed while the pupil is in the elementary school, and his educational habits are formed here. More teaching ability is needed with pupils of immature age, and therefore more careful supervision of the work of education. Care must also be exercised to see that the work is unified and correlated as the pupil passes from grade to grade and from teacher to teacher.

Departments. As elementary schools are usually organized there are three distinct departments, the Primary Department of three years, the Intermediate Deparment of three years, and the Grammar Department of two years. Sometimes there is also a Kindergarten Department of one year, preceding the Primary Department.

Each department, to a degree, is distinct in its aim and in its method. When the school is organized under the Junior-Senior plan, the Grammar Department becomes a part of the Junior High School or Intermediate School, which somewhat modifies its purpose and method.

The Kindergarten. This department does not concern the officials of the small school system, as it is not practical here to attempt to maintain a Kindergarten Department. There is not usually an available room, nor are there pupils enough for such department. The work requires the services of a specially qualified teacher. It is impractical to try to combine this with Primary work. A few schools have attempted this, but the effort has resulted instead in a Sub-Primary grade, which has no practical function. Such schools are fast eliminating the Sub-Primary year. Pupils usually enter the Kindergarten at five years of age, although in some districts they may enter younger. The distinct purpose of the Kindergarten is to bridge over the transition of the child from the home to the school and to give a certain training which neither provides. Here the child becomes gradually accustomed to school environment and to school methods. He learns to obey requests and to follow directions. He finds how to mingle with other children and to co-operate in games, etc. Certain games, construction and general matters are learned. Sense training is emphasized, and primary concepts in morals, religion, ethics, citizenship, etc., are established. The Kindergarten teacher, by nature, should be both a mother and an older sister. To be most successful she should have also some attributes of a nurse. It is better if the Kindergarten room is somewhat isolated from the other departments of the school. It should be emphasized that for a Kindergarten full equipment should be provided, and a specially prepared teacher be employed.

The Primary Department.   This includes pupils from five to eight years of age.   The department consists of three years of work above the Kindergarten, with the emphasis placed upon the subject of Reading.   The securing of a vocabulary and the development of expression constitute the chief ends to be sought.   Sense training and ability in construction are important.   Primary concepts in the various subjects are developed as a basis for future work, although Number work, Nature study, etc., are taught incidentally and usually without a text in hands of pupils.   Phonics and Spelling are emphasized in connection with the Reading work.   During the first two years, at least, a method reader with appropriate charts and cards should be used.   The Primary teacher usually uses chart and blackboard, only, for the reading work, for a period of six to eight weeks.   Two Primers and two First Readers constitute a reasonable standard for the first year of work in reading, one First Reader and three Second Readers for the second year and four Third Readers for the third year.   Except for the Basic reader, the readers may be chosen for their content. The Basic reader should be the first reader used each year.   Usually the pupils furnish the Basic reader and the district furnishes sets of the others as supplementary. As it is sometimes difficult to have pupils get texts promptly there is some advantage in the district furnishing all the readers in the Primary department.   It is well for each grade here to be supplied with a reader set designed distinctly for dramatic reading.

Primary teachers should be specially trained in Primary methods, and it is, of course, preferred that they have some Primary experience.   Especially is the training necessary for a teacher in the First Primary grade.

The Intermediate Department. This department in general includes pupils from eight to eleven years of age and consists of grades four, five and six. While Reading here is also an important subject, other subjects are carried, with texts in the hands of pupils. The Number Work of the Primary department becomes Arithmetic, and Nature Study is replaced by Geography. Written work is here taken up in earnest, and the writing of examinations begun. The use of the dictionary should begin in the Fourth grade or the Fifth grade, and teachers should give especial training to pupils in proper use of dictionary. Three readers should be read by each grade. Not so much attention need be paid to Basic reader as formerly. One reader chosen may be designed especially to develop the power of silent reading.

This is an important department from the standpoint of inculcating habits of study and methods of work. The grades in this department should neither be ignored nor slighted. Teachers should be well prepared and adapted to children of this age. It is, of course, better if the teachers should have had previous experience.

The Grammar Department. This department consists of two years of work, the Seventh and Eighth grades. The ages in general range from twelve to fourteen. As this touches the pre-adolescent period of childhood it is considered a difficult department. All the elementary subjects here receive attention, and pupils complete, in this department, the range or content of the so-called "common branches." The work differs from that of the Intermediate department in being less simple. The subject matter becomes more organized and reference to helps outside the text is used. Organizations may be made a strong factor and a help to the work.

The Grammar department is important as an opportunity to interest pupils in subjects beyond the elementary school and hold them in school for high school work. In some schools each grade will be in a separate room, although it is no disadvantage, providing the grades are not too large, to have both grades with the same teacher. The Grammar room teacher should have more scholastic preparation than is required of other grade teachers. She should be strong in discipline, which means that she should understand and sympathize with boys and girls of Grammar school age. Usually a mature teacher succeeds better here, although sometimes a young teacher does remarkably well.

General Suggestions on the Elementary Work

(a) No teacher should have more than three grades, preferably not more than two grades.

(b) When a teacher has but one grade the grade should be sectioned, if there are more than fifteen pupils in the grade, and in most subjects the sections should recite separately, to allow more opportunity for participation by individual pupils.

(c) In dividing a grade into two sections care should be exercised that some of the stronger ones and some of the weaker ones be placed in each section; that is, that the two sections approximately average in ability to do the work. In large schools where semi-annual promotions are possible a plan may safely be used of dividing a grade according to ability. In sectioning a grade it is better not to designate divisions as "1" and "2" or as "a" and "b." Some distinctive name may better be given each division which does not carry the idea of superiority or inferiority.

(d) Subjects in which both sections may well participate at the same time in recitation are: Penmanship, Drawing, Music, Spelling and occasionally in assigning or developing certain lessons in other subjects. Some general lessons on Health, Morals, Nature Study and Citizenship may well be taught to both sections simultaneously.

(e) When a grade is sectioned, care should be exercised that one division does not prepare its lessons by listening to the recitation of the previous division. This can be avoided by assigning, daily, slightly different lessons to the different divisions, or by having one division several lessons in advance of the other.

(f) In making a program for a room, a definite study period, as well as a recitation period, should be indicated, at least below the Seventh grade, and this schedule should be posted in a conspicuous place in the room. The superintendent also should have in his office a copy of each room program. In the Sixth, Seventh and Eighth grades a good plan is to have the study period of a subject follow immediately after the recitation period for that subject.

(g) In the "Beginning Class" in the Primary department, owing to the varying age and ability of the pupils, division may well be made according to ability. The slower pupils should be the smaller section, as these pupils can then be given more individual attention.

(h) Except in schools where semi-annual promotions are possible, a "Beginning Class" should be organized only at the first of the school year. It is not necessary to allow "Beginning" pupils to enroll whenever their fifth birthday occurs, or at any time later than the first two weeks of the school year, and such enrollment is usually demoralizing to the work of the Primary teacher.

(i) The practice of providing a sub-primary year or "Beginning" year, previous to the First grade work, is generally being discontinued, except when a regular Kindergarten department can be maintained with a specially trained Kindergarten teacher.

(j) Usually an intermission period, both forenoon and afternoon, should be rigidly adhered to below the High School, or at least below the Grammar School.

(k) During the intermission period it is equally unwise to allow a pupil to remain in the room in good weather or to force him to spend the period outside in inclement weather, or when he does not feel well.

(l) The playground should be supervised, but the play is often better if not directed. The purpose of supervision is to prevent serious friction, bad language, rough sports, and to see that no child is left out of the games. Teachers may well be assigned to playground supervision, a day at a time or a week at a time, in their turn.

(m) Discussion of current events once or twice per week should be held in the Grammar School and in the Sixth grade. A few good magazines in the school are a valuable aid.

(n) Below the Seventh grade the reading work should be confined mostly to method readers and to content readers. Pupils in the first six grades need the variety of readings given in regular readers, to introduce them to various life interests.

(o) Classics may be used for Reading work in the Grammar department, instead of readers. Complete units will thus be given.

(p) In general the smaller school systems should not

attempt semi-annual promotions, especially if there
be more than one grade in a room.

(q) The true term to use for children in the elementary school is "pupil," not "student" nor "scholar."

(r) The major emphasis on subjects varies as follows:

1. Primary Department — English and Nature
Study groups.

2. Intermediate Department — Arithmetic and
Science groups.

3. Grammar Department—Social Science, or History and Civics groups.

Organization of the High School. The age of high
school students usually ranges from fourteen to eighteen
years, and covers the complete adolescent period. The
High School as usually classified consists of four years of
work above eight years of elementary work. The grades
are known as Ninth grade, Tenth grade, Eleventh grade
and Twelfth grade. To distinguish this plan from the
Junior-Senior High School, it is sometimes designated as
the 8-4 plan. Another plan is the Junior-Senior, or 6-3-3
plan, six years of elementary work, three years of Junior
high school work and three years of Senior high school
work. Still another plan is the 6-2-4 plan, or the Elementary-Intermediate-High School plan. The Intermediate School here takes the place of the Grammar Department.

The High School course of study is always differen-
tiated from the Elementary course. The true Junior-
Senior high school or the true Elementary-Intermediate-
High School plan reorganizes the Seventh and Eighth
Grade Course. Small schools have difficulty in reorgan-
izing on either of these bases, and unless the organiza-
tion can be carried out completely it is of doubtful value.
The main difficulties are:

1. Buildings are not usually so arranged as to provide two high school rooms, and it is not wise to place the six higher grades in one room, owing to the wide disparity in ages and in interests.

2. Unless the two rooms are located in close proximity it means the duplicating of library and equipment.

3. It calls for better qualified and therefore higher salaried teachers for the Seventh and the Eighth grades.

4. Usually the small school system has rural pupils entering the Ninth grade. These would not have had the same work as the town pupils, in Seventh and Eighth grades, hence would not be fitted to work together with them in the Ninth grade. The larger high school might section classes to obviate this difficulty. The plan is more feasible for the consolidated school than for the small town school, because the consolidated school does not usually enroll non-resident pupils.

The high school differs from the elementary school also in the matter of promotions. In the former the student is promoted by subjects, while in the latter the pupil is promoted by grades, or credits. Four subjects constitute regular work in each grade of the high school. A student should not be permitted to take fewer subjects unless from necessity, and seldom should be allowed to take more than the regular number.

General Suggestions on the High School Work

(a) The plan of four forty-minute or forty-five-minute periods in the forenoon and four in the afternoon makes the best arrangement in the small high school, as this gives approximately half the time to students for preparation of lessons.

(b) In Science subjects, two double periods weekly

should be used for experiments and demonstrations. With real small classes this may not always be necessary.

(c) Teachers should be assigned work as far as possible to conform to the following:

1. Ability to handle subject matter, as shown by special preparation, previous experience or natural ability.

2. To bring each teacher in direct class contact with as many of the student body as possible.

3. According to disciplinary ability. Young and inexperienced teachers in general should be given the classes more easily managed.

4. To give each teacher, as far as possible, most of her work along her special line; but a subject or two out of her special line is often wholesome for both teacher and school.

(d) Discussion of current events should be had once or twice per week, either in recitation or in general exercises. Whichever plan is used it should reach every student. A few weekly or monthly magazines should be provided.

(e) General opening exercises may be held once per week. Many teachers use this period for singing and devotionals.

(f) One teacher should be charged especially with the care of the high school library. All teachers should direct students in the use of books in the library. In a large high school the teacher in charge of the library should have some special library training. This training may be obtained by attendance at a suitable summer school.

(g) To increase the interest and maintain the morale of the high school the formation of one or more organizations is good, such as Literary Societies, Athletic Associations, or Glee Clubs. Whatever organizations are maintained should be democratic, should avoid tendency to professionalism and should be wholly under control of the superintendent or teacher appointed by him. Contests within the school by classes or organizations are more desirable than contests with neighboring schools.

(h) Class organizations should not be encouraged below the Junior year, and in small high schools the value of class organizations at all is doubtful.

(i) Classes or organizations should clearly understand that funds raised from public entertainments, etc., belong to the school and not to the class or to the organization. The Board of Education may, if it so desires, permit the class or other organization to choose the method of expenditure of such receipts for the school, but the fund does not belong to the **organization** nor to the individuals of the organization.

(j) The class of entertainments to be fostered by a high school organization should be first sanctioned by the superintendent and the principal, and in general should be of such nature that all members may conscientiously take part.

(k) As an occasional class exercise, school exercise or in business meetings of the high school organizations, the students should be instructed and drilled in simple parliamentary rules.

(l) In keeping record of credits earned by students, some system should be used that will show on one page, by year, all credits of a student for the full high school course. Special forms for such can be secured from most school supply houses. This record is **very** important and should be kept in permanent form in the office of the school superintendent or in the files of the secretary to the Board of Education.

(m) Any teacher in the high school may legitimately be called upon to take charge of assembly room, do hall duty, etc.

CHAPTER VII

Class-Room Organization

Scope. Although the term "Class-Room" is in general not clearly defined, it is here used to denote a room in which one or more classes or grades sit for study, or for both study and recitation purposes. The discussion here applies more to the grade room, but may, in part, apply also to the high school study room or to the high school recitation room.

Seating of Pupils. An important matter in class-room organization is the proper seating of pupils. Although no definite rule can be given to apply to all schools or to all rooms, a few matters for consideration will here be given, and in the order of first importance.

1. Pupils, above all, should be so seated that the desks and the seats are suited to them in the matter of height. The pupil's feet should reach the floor comfortably and without elevating the knees or without compelling the pupil's limbs to be extended. The desk should be just high enough for the pupils to assume a good writing position. When adjustable seats and desks are provided these should be carefully adjusted with the pupil sitting, and the adjustment should be made both at the beginning of the school year and again in the middle of the school year.

2. Children delicate in health should be so located as to avoid cold parts of the room or sudden draughts. Pupils with poor eyesight should be in close proximity to black-boards, charts, etc., while those with defective hearing should be near the front of the room.

3. There are usually in each room two or more grades or sections; usually a section or grade is seated together

on one side of the room. If the room has regular recitation seats and pupils are inclined to assist each other too much, it may be wise to scatter the sections promiscuously to avoid this.

4. Communicative and troublesome pupils may be isolated from other pupils or seated near the front of the room under close supervision of the teacher.

Organization of Pupils' Work. A few schools, especially in Kindergarten and Primary rooms, use study tables instead of individual desks. This eliminates the rigid, static condition of the room and permits more freedoom to the pupils. When the regular individual seat and desk are used for each pupil, the desk becomes the pupil's "office", and he may be taught to have office system and office rules. Regular office hours may be scheduled and office routine observed. The pupil then feels personally responsible for the condition of the office and for the proper keeping of books and papers.

Some schools have monthly inspection of the pupils' text books by principal or teacher, to induce better care of books. The teacher's care of desk and books should be a model for the pupils. Each text, tablet and pencil box kept by the pupil should have a definite place in the desk. The proper use of tablets should be taught, or many pupils are apt to be wasteful and slovenly with them. Some teachers have pupils in a class procure the same kind of permanent tablet, have these tablets carefully paged, and then hold pupils responsible for use of each page.

The Schedule. The very first day of the year or the semester, if possible, there should be arranged a definite time schedule for both recitations and study periods. In the Grammar room and the High School it is, of course, not so necessary for students to adhere to a definite study hour, although there is distinct advantage to a student in having a definite routine of work. In the High School it is usually considered that the study period for a regular academic subject should be twice the length of the recitation period, except where laboratory periods are added to recitation periods. In general, a grade schedule, at least below Seventh grade, should provide equal length of recitation periods and study periods.

In Intermediate and in Grammar departments some teachers claim much better results by having the study period follow immediately the recitation period in a given subject. This permits pupils to prepare an assignment while it is clearly in mind and when interest in the subject is aroused.

During a study period, pupils may be allowed to read current magazines or library reference books for remainder of period after the preparation of the lesson is complete. This is an inducement to concentrated attention and rapid work. At the same time it may lead to careless work or "skimming", so should be watched carefully. The reading of stories in school should usually not be permitted, as such practice is apt to dissipate attention to lessons.

In the daily schedule there should be provided a period of from ten to twenty minutes for general exercises. Except in the Primary department one such period per day is sufficient. Usually this exercise is scheduled at the beginning of either the forenoon or the afternoon session, although a few teachers prefer it at the close of the session as a relaxation. The general exercise should be purposeful, either instructive or inspirational in character, not simply entertaining. Sometimes it may be used for some lively drill. A singing exercise is excellent if well conducted and not overdone. Usually there is no objection to the use of devotionals, although care on the part of the teacher should be exercised that no pupil be offended by requiring him to take part in religious exercises to which he or his parents might object. The giving of quotations by pupils is good. In upper grades and in high school, one period per week may well be used in discussion of "current events". Here, also, an outside speaker, singer, etc., may be utilized. The exercise should be spirited and not become a bore to pupils. For this reason the exercise should be varied occasionally.

The daily schedule should be carefully followed as to time, although recitation work may be varied. It is not always necessary that at each recitation period pupils recite. Sometimes drill work may be the order during this period, and occasionally a full recitation period may be given over to review or to assignment of an important lesson.

The Recitation. In general, the purpose of the recitation is fourfold, to test the pupils' preparation of the assignment, to review the previous lesson, to correlate or give added information to connect the lesson with previous lessons, and to create interest in future lessons by carefully making the following day's assignment. At times, also, drill of fundamentals becomes an important purpose. It is not necessary, of course, that these purposes always be considered in their order, nor that all of them be recognized in every recitation. Sometimes one may predominate and at other times others, or one may at certain times command all the attention in the recitation. It is important, however, that the teacher's preparation for the recitation shall be considered in all these relations.

The place and manner of holding the recitation are more important than usually considered. A separate recitation room provided with blackboard, charts and other helps is ideal. Where one teacher does all the work of the room and there are more than one section or grade, this is practically impossible of attainment. The next better plan is to have separate recitation seats, either in the front or in the rear of the room. Either of these conditions permit the changing of environment, which is psychologically a help in getting pupils in the attitude of mind for a recitation. When pupils must, however, remain at their individual desks for the recitation, it is a good plan, before beginning the recitation work, to have pupils stand and take breathing or calisthenic exercises for a moment or two, or even to march around the room. This gets the mind off the study and secures attention on the recitation.

Further mention will be made regarding the manner of conducting the recitation, but mention may be made here of the importance of promptness and order. If pupils are required to stand to recite, they should stand erect and a little away from the desk. No books, pencils, etc., should be on the desk to invite fumbling.

Blackboard Work. Although blackboard work is often a part of the recitation, it is considered here of enough importance for separate consideration. Every class-room and every recitation room should have plenty of blackboard space, with the board properly placed. There should be board space in a recitation room for the maximum number of students to work at once. In a grade or class-room the board space should accommodate one-half the number of pupils in the room. Usually it is better not to have the blackboard placed in the rear of the room, but rather in the front and on one or two sides. The blackboard is often used by the teacher for assignment of problems and other work, and this should be carefully placed and written large enough so that all pupils may see the work without eye strain. The front board is usually used for this purpose, to avoid the necessity of pupils turning to see the work.

Some teachers question the value of pupils using the blackboard, especially in the Primary department. Primary pupils enjoy blackboard work, however, and there seems to be no valid reason why they may not use the board as soon as they begin to draw or write. For all pupils a blackboard exercise offers variety in the work, and any teacher knows a school ordinarily has too little variety. Excellent lessons of order, neatness, etc., may also be taught at the blackboard, which cannot be taught as well elsewhere. An excellent opportunity is here offered for criticism by all members of the class. Board work in this way places individual responsibility of a high order, and if combined with demonstration by the pupil is exceedingly educative in its process.

In blackboard work, during recitation period, usually all members of the class should participate, if there is room. The blackboard should be thoroughly erased before the exercise begins. No margin of crayon marks should surround the space used by a pupil. When work is assigned it is better that all begin work at the same time. Sometimes it is preferable to assign the work before the pupils pass to the board. In assigning problems, topics or exercises, not all should be given the same, for there is too much inducement to copy or to compare. Problems may be assigned in alternation, or the class may number by ones, twos, threes, etc., to receive their assigned exercise. The work should be inspected by the teacher before being erased, and mistakes corrected. Slovenly work should be required to be rewritten. Work should not be erased until the signal is given. Order should prevail in board work. At close of the blackboard exercise all work should be carefully erased unless there is a definite purpose for its remaining. All work should be neat, accurate and rapid. A drone or a slovenly worker may, as a punishment, be prohibited the use of the blackboard for a season. If there is not room for all members of the class to work at the board, those at the recitation seat should be given work to do there. They may each be appointed to follow the work of a certain pupil at the board and offer corrections or criticisms.

Method of Questioning. In conducting a recitation much depends upon the art of questioning. The teacher should be so familiar with the subject in hand and so definite in the purpose to be accomplished that she will need no open text book as an aid. Much better results will be obtained if no help of this kind is at hand for the teacher during the recitation. As soon as teachers become accustomed to conducting a recitation without text or notes they invariably prefer this to any other plan.

Space will not permit, in this discussion, more than a few points to be considered. Moreover, this is a discussion on organization rather than on methods, so a lengthy discussion would have no place here. Several methods of questioning should be noticed, however, such as the question and answer method, the answer being "yes" or "no", or by the use of the indirect question method, the topic method in which pupils are asked to recite by topics studied in the text. A third method is to discuss a certain phase of the subject, requesting such a discussion by one pupil as fully as possible and then by a general discussion by other members of the class. Still another plan is to have pupils bring questions to the recitation to be answered by other members of the class or by the teacher. All of these methods have their merits, and probably no one method should be used exclusively.

Some recitations resolve themselves into drill exercises, naturally, in which pupils, one at a time, go through the exercise, or all go through the exercise in concert. If pupils are called upon individually to recite, it is usually better that they are called promiscuously rather than in order as they are seated or alphabetically by name. Better attention on the part of all can thus be secured. Again, the pupil's name should be called after the question is asked or the topic assigned rather than before. The reason for this is obvious. It is often discussed as to whether a teacher should require pupils to stand during a recitation exercise, that is,—while the pupil is reciting. Most teachers prefer this in the grades, but do not insist upon it in the high school. More responsibility is placed upon the pupil if he stands before the class in recitation and it is not so easy for him to refuse to recite if he must stand and fail to answer a question or to recite on a topic. It is much more embarrassing than if he simply refuses while seated. In rapid review exercises it is probably better to permit pupils to remain seated. Primary teachers often prefer to have pupils stand during the whole recitation exercise.

Assignment of Lesson. Mention has been made that one of the purposes of the recitation period is the assignment of the following lesson. This is so important that it needs separate consideration. In Primary and Intermediate departments it is usually better that the assignment be made just before the study period for a subject, as pupils can then better know just what to do in the preparation. In the upper grades or the high school, however, the assignment should usually be made at the time of the recitation or during the recitation period.

Many teachers prefer to make the assignment at the beginning of the recitation period rather than at the close, so that they may not be hurried in the assignment. Whenever the assignment is made, sufficient time should be given to make the matter clear to all pupils, and they should then be held responsible for such preparation. They should not be permitted to acquire the habit of inquiring again concerning the assignment.

In the assignment of a lesson it is not enough for the teacher to say "take the next lesson", or "take so many pages". This is no assignment at all. The assignment should be so definite that pupils may know for just what they are to be held accountable in the recitation. If work outside the text is assigned, this should also be definite and pupils should be told where to find the material. The proper assignment of a lesson necessarily requires previous preparation on the part of the teacher. Some teachers keep a daily plan book or weekly plan book in which assignment of all lessons are carefully written out. This is an excellent practice, especially by an inexperienced teacher. It is not too much to say that at least one-half the success of a recitation depends upon the previous assignment of the lesson by the teacher. Unless a teacher makes careful assignment of a lesson she should not complain of pupils who come to recitation partially prepared.

The Matter of Discipline. A whole chapter more than once has been written on the subject of discipline, but a few suggestions may be ventured here. There is much confusion in the understanding of the term "discipline". In the minds of many teachers it means simply "punishment". It should mean "training", and in this sense every pupil should be disciplined every day he is in school.

Two opposite theories obtain at present concerning so-called school discipline. One theory is that there should be almost military order in and about the school room; that pupils should be taught to obey implicity and at once and be properly punished for disobedience. This theory is giving place to a milder form of discipline, however, and some educators go to the extent of advocating self-discipline by the pupil, or much freedom of action by the child. Out of this has grown what is known to be "student self-government" or "student co-operative government". No doubt some good can be said for each of these methods, but probably the successful method lies between these two extremes. No doubt pupils may be given much self-determination in the matter of their actions if this be given them gradually, as they are able to assume such. With Primary and Intermediate children not so much self-government can be granted as to those in the Grammar school and the High School. In any department, leadership rather than autocracy ought to be the motto of the teacher. Whatever form of government, the teacher should be leader and be the responsible head in the room. The success of any method of discipline depends upon the teacher's personality and leadership rather than on the method.

Discipline should obtain not only in the school room, but in passing to and from the school room, in activities on the playground, and even in the social relations of pupils on the way to and from school. It should even carry further and govern the pupils in their actions at home and on the street. The influence of the discipline in the school should "carry over" to other activities and environments.

Much of the success of a teacher in the government of her pupils in the school room depends upon her supervision of the child's activities on the playground. Careful supervision here will prevent many troubles elsewhere. Some teachers have a system of using monitors or assistants in the school. While this may sometimes be justifiable, it is not to be recommended, as it often creates jealousy among pupils and becomes a temptation to the teacher to shift responsibility.

A question always discussed but never yet settled is the question of whether pupils shall be permitted to communicate, or whisper, in school. It is safe to say that there are very few school rooms in which there is not some such communicating done, in some rooms, no doubt, too much of it. No definite rule can be made. No doubt communicating can be placed on a basis of fairness and yet within control of the teacher. One successful teacher has a rule that no pupil shall whisper to another pupil in the room unless he leave his own desk and stand beside the desk of the pupil to whom he wishes to speak. If the communication becomes prolonged or accorded too frequently, the privilege is taken away from such pupil for a certain period of time. This plan no doubt has its merits.

Another puzzling question for the teacher is to know whether to permit one pupil to assist another pupil in work. It is true that outside the school room, in all activities of life, children are urged to be helpful, one to another. It, therefore, may not be wise to absolutely prohibit this help in the school, but every teacher knows it must be controlled or some pupils would give too much help and others would be glad to receive too much help. It is really an individual matter for each teacher to decide.

In closing this discussion, one other point ought perhaps to be considered. There has grown up in our schools a system of contests and rewards much greater than schools formerly had. The granting of half-holidays, exemption from examinations, a place on the roll

of honor, etc., has, in some schools, become pernicious in
its results as a whole on the school. Weaker pupils are
discouraged because they cannot hope to obtain a place
of honor, while stronger pupils come to feel that there is
no inducement to good work without some kind of re-
ward. The idea of good work for the work's sake and
for the reaction on the pupil in the feeling of having done
good work is lost. Pupils are in this way incidentally
taught to believe that good work merits exemption or a
shortening of the period of work.

CHAPTER VIII

Administration of the School

Types of Teachers Needed. The several departments of the school have been discussed in regard to organization and type of work. A word may here be given relative to choice of teachers for each department. Children of the various departments differ in age and nature, hence require a different type of teacher. A few teachers there are who are born teachers and can adapt themselves to any age or department. Many there are who are somewhat naturally adapted to succeed with certain ages of pupils. These will succeed, if rightly placed, but will become mediocre teachers or worse if placed in the wrong department. Another class of teachers become teachers by training only, therefore should be placed in the work for which they are specially trained. The special training must always be taken into account in placing teachers, and usually receives first consideration.

Kindergarten and Primary children need a teacher with mother instinct, one who will in a measure take the place of the mother in the home. For this reason some contend that a Kindergarten or a Primary teacher should be mature in age. Many young teachers, however, succeed here, just as young nurses succeed well in caring for children. It is not a matter of age, but a matter of understanding and sympathy. The Intermediate pupil does not so much need a mother as an older sister. The teacher should be a child leader, able to direct pupils in games and sports as well as in regular school work. The Grammar Room teacher, on the other hand, should be somewhat of a commander, a benevolent ruler. She should understand the meaning of adolescent age and should have a controlling and steadying influence over those in her charge.   The High School teacher should be somewhat of a companion and an organizer, and at the same time she should have social discretion and mature judgment.

In visiting numerous schools one will be impressed by the fact that in general the younger teachers are found in the High School department, many of these with very little or with no experience.   On the other hand, the older and the most experienced teachers are in general found teaching the grade work.   While an economic or a professional explanation may be found for this, in some ways it seems unfortunate.   Youth in the high school especially need the steadying influence and the wise direction that comes from mature leadership and experience in life problems.

There is a general opinion that the Grammar department is the most important and the most difficult to teach.   From one standpoint this may be true, that of keeping pupils in school.   The compulsory school age ends here and there is a "Call to the Market Place".   In all departments there are problems which can be solved only by an understanding, appreciative and sympathetic teacher.   The Kindergarten and Primary departments are more simple and lend themselves more readily to special method in the work.

General Notes on Administration

(a) When possible, a small office with desk and filing case should be provided for the superintendent.   A roll-top desk or a flat-top desk with plenty of drawers, placed in the assembly room, is the best substitute for an office.   The superintendent, however, should spend but little time in his office during school hours.

(b) The superintendent should, if possible, visit each teacher's work at least once a week, and often for a full recitation period. To avoid visiting the same recitation each time, he can ask the teacher to vary her program for the day.

(c) After a visit to a room or recitation, the superintended should, at his earliest convenience, discuss the work with the teacher. He should tactfully suggest improvements and in general assist the teacher in a constructive way.

(d) When the superintendent has entire charge of a room and cannot visit, he should have a weekly conference with each teacher regarding her work.

(e) The superintendent should hold a general teachers' meeting at least once per month for conference on school work or for study of methods.

(f) Examinations are held above the Primary department in some schools once per month, in others once in six weeks, and in still others once in nine weeks. The six-weeks' period seems best for the small school.

(g) There is a growing tendency to promote pupils in class-room standing more than on result of examination. Many schools count two-thirds on the former and one-third on the latter.

(h) Teachers may well be required to arrive at the building thirty minutes before the opening of school at the morning session and fifteen minutes previous at the afternoon session.

(i) Pupils should never be left alone in the building at the noon period. If a responsible janitor is not in charge, teachers and superintendent should take their turn daily or weekly in taking personal charge at this time.

(j) In two-story or three-story buildings systematic fire drill should be held once per month or oftener.

(k) Much time in some schools is wasted by purposeless "opening exercises", especially in the grades. Except in Primary grades it is not necessary to have two periods per day for such exercises. "Opening Exercises" should be instructive or inspirational rather than entertaining.

(1) A superintendent should not assume hall duty, but should assign such to teachers, as his time should be free for more general duties. This does not signify that he should shift responsibility for order and discipline.

(m) Departmental teaching is being successfully used in some Grammar Schools, but it does not seem advisable to attempt such below the Seventh grade.

(n) The superintendent should supervise the daily records kept by teachers and carefully examine all reports made out by them.

(o) General supervision of the work in vocational and other special subjects should not be neglected by the superintendent. These should be made practical and should, as far as possible, be correlated with the other work of the school.

(p) Where old, out-of-date texts are in use, these should be changed gradually for modern texts. The change should be made at the close rather than during the school year, and always with the privilege of exchanging displaced books for new adoptions at the usual rate of exchange. When a text covers two years of work it is well the first year to make the exchange only in the beginning class in the subject and complete the adoption of the new text the second year. Adoption of a text must always be by formal action of the Board of Education, and should be on the recommendation of the superintendent.

(q) Some general supplies are usually furnished by the district instead of being purchased by pupils, such as construction paper, drawing paper, pens, ink, and sometimes penmanship practice paper and examination paper. Usually, schools furnish also half the Readers in the grades, as supplementary sets, and some furnish sets of Music and Drawing books for each grade.

(r) Owing to the arrangement of the building some schools find it necessary or expedient to seat the Grammar School with the High School. In such case, a good recitation plan is to make the Grammar School recitation periods equal in time to the High School periods and use the last ten or fifteen minutes of the period for study of the following day's assignment.

(s) Regular monthly meetings of the Board of Education should be encouraged, and the superintendent should attend each meeting. At these meetings the superintendent should report the progress of the school and make needed recommendations.

(t) The superintendent of a small school, as well as the superintendent of a larger school system, should assume the duties of a superintendent as far as his time permits. He should seek to train his inexperienced teachers in service and assign general duties. In employment of teachers he should be consulted by the Board of Education, and he should have general administrative and supervisory control of the school.

(u) While the organization of the High School department calls for more teachers for the same sized group of pupils than in the Elementary departments, owing to laboratory periods and longer recitation periods, care should be exercised that the school shall not be made top-heavy. In some schools as many teachers are found employed for the high school as for the grades, when there is but one-fourth the enrollment in the high school.

(v) While in the small school system the superintendent must teach classes in the High School department, he should not allow his interest to center on this department to the neglect of the grade work.

(w) The usual length of the school year is nine months, extending from the first Monday in September until about the last of May. Usually one or two weeks of vacation are given during the Christmas holiday season and sometimes one week at Easter time. Some schools prefer not to have a Spring vacation, as it induces older pupils to withdraw from school to work. A few schools employ teachers for nine and one-half months, making the school year that long. For holidays and examination days about ten days of time are taken from the regular school work, so by this plan nine months of school in the clear is left.

(x) Schools are often hampered by closing of school at time of epidemic. Sometimes this may be necessary, but more often not necessary. Some schools, to prevent closing of school for contagious disease, have organized at such times as follows:

1. Have a physician or nurse explain to assembled teachers how to discern symptoms of children affected by the disease.

2. Have each teacher observant and send home any suspected pupil. The pupil must then present a physician's certificate of freedom from the disease, when returning. When a child is sent home thus, the health physician is immediately notified.

3. No child from a home where there is sickness is allowed in school without a physician's certificate that the sickness is not of a contagious nature.

4. Whenever a pupil is absent from school, the health physician is notified and the pupil not al-

lowed to return without an examination by a physician or a nurse.

The advocates of this plan claim it is more effective in controlling a contagious disease, as all suspicious cases are thus discovered and investigated where they would not be discovered if school were not in session.

(y) How to prevent tardiness and absence is always a problem. Two methods are used to deal with the problem:

1. In case of absence or tardiness, the pupil is required to present a written excuse from the parent. It is difficult to prevent bogus excuses being used, and again, some delinquent children find it easy to obtain excuses from the indulgent parent.

2. In case of absence or tardiness, to require a written excuse from the superintendent. In case of doubt, the superintendent can require his written excuse to be countersigned by the parent.

(z) The matter of punishment is a delicate one. Most state laws permit a teacher to inflict corporal punishment, although a Board of Education may prohibit it locally. Some "Boards" allow the superintendent, but not the teachers, to use such punishment. Some schools establish the rule that no teacher may inflict corporal punishment on a pupil except in the presence of another teacher or the superintendent.

CHAPTER IX

The Problem of Supervision

The subject of supervision in a system of schools is of so much importance that it seems to merit a separate discussion. Of the three functions to perform devolving upon the executive head of a school system, organization is the first to consider, since this must be established first of all. Work should be well organized before it can properly function. After being organized, however, not much attention need be centered upon this function. Administration, the second function in school management, has to do with general duties in matters of the school. Organization is creating a machine and administration is running the machine. Supervision, however, the last to consider, might be compared to feeding the machine and examining the product. This must receive constant attention so long as the machine is running. Supervision is the real professional end of school management and is the real test of a good superintendent.

The Measure of Efficiency. No doubt the greatest lack in proper school management on the part of the superintendent is found in the matter of supervision. This may not be the fault of the superintendent, since often his duties are so numerous that he does not have time to properly supervise the work of his school. In a small school system much of his time is taken up with instruction in the high school department. This work, together with the general administrative duties, occupies so much of his time that he can not properly supervise his school. He should, however, so systematize his work that he may be able to supervise the work of each teacher enough, at least, to have an intelligent understanding of the work being done. The minimum should be the visiting of each teacher's classroom work one recitation period per week. In a small school system employing not more than a dozen teachers, where the superintendent may come in daily contact with teachers in the building, this one period is probably sufficient. No teacher should be entirely slighted and, on the other hand, supervision by an inexperienced superintendent may be overdone, since the teacher understands the work of her department better than the superintendent does.

The inexperienced superintendent in visiting a classroom should not attempt too much direction of the work, but should learn from his experienced teacher the purpose and method of the work conducted. Gradually he will become able to offer some suggestions of value, but he should not assume that it is a duty in every case to offer suggestions or criticisms.

Method of Supervision. It has been suggested that the superintendent should visit the classroom of each teacher one period per week as a minimum. At times it may be valuable for him to be in the room during the study period or the period of general exercises as well, so that he may get an idea of how all the work is being conducted. Some time during the day, after such a visit, the superintendent should seek opportunity to confer with the teacher regarding the work observed. He may properly ask questions concerning the purpose of this or that method employed, the ability of this or that pupil, etc. The first thing he should seek is information regarding the work the teacher has in charge.

Occasionally there is a superintendent who thinks it is his duty in supervising the work of a classroom to take charge of the class exercise and conduct it himself so as to show the teacher his method of presenting the lesson. This is a dangerous thing to do, especially if the teacher is experienced and the superintendent inexperienced, and it is usually not at all necessary. In general, a superintendent in visiting a classroom should keep himself in the background so as not unduly to attract the attention of the pupils. In this way the work will proceed more normally, and that is what the superintendent desires, in order to get a true measure of the work.

Not all the supervision work of a superintendent, however, is done in the classroom. He sometimes writes examination questions for the students and reviews the examination papers after they have been graded by the teacher. This is an excellent way to find out the ability of the pupils and the painstaking care of the teacher in the matter of this written work. Again a good plan is to require teachers to prepare a daily or weekly plan book of recitations. This is a benefit to the teachers as well as to the superintendent. The superintendent should also examine class record books and class registers to see that they are carefully kept.

Another effective means of keeping in touch with the work of the different departments is the holding of regular meetings of teachers. These are usually held after school or in the evening for an hour, monthly or semi-monthly. These meetings may be given over to discussion of local school problems or for a study of methods of presenting the work. Occasionally it may be well for the meeting to be turned into a social meeting. In a smaller system of schools it is urgent that all the teachers meet together in these meetings instead of the meetings being held in groups. This brings the teachers into contact and places them in their true relation to the system. The superintendent should preside at all such meetings.

Points to Observe in Classroom Supervision. In entering a classroom the superintendent's attention will naturally be directed to many things. A few are here mentioned as being of decided importance.

1. The superintendent should note the material aspects of the room, that is, to discover whether things are in order or whether the room presents a slovenly and disordered appearance.

2. The personal appearance of both teacher and pupils should be noticed. The superintendent should not be too critical on these points, of course, but if the pupils are accustomed to appear in the school room with uncombed hair, with slovenly attire, etc., this should be called to the attention of the teacher and steps taken to remedy the matter. However, the teacher may sometimes be open to criticism in the matter of her dress and this, of course, must be criticised in a tactful way.

3. The deportment of the room should receive attention. This does not mean that there should be no noise, but that there should not be confusion or purposeful mischief discernible. The true school atmosphere shows a busy attitude on the part of all concerned. Interest in study or in the class exercise should prevail.

4. The personality of the teacher should be taken into account. Her manner of speaking to the pupils and her power of leadership are important. The teacher should be a leader in all the work of the room.

5. The superintendent should note whether the teacher has initiative in her work or is simply copying in her method of handling it. Severe criticism sometimes inhibits initiative on the part of the teacher, and the super-

intendent should be careful to encourage initiative rather than to prohibit it.

6. Preparation of the teacher for her daily work as evidenced by her manner of conducting the recitation and the assignment of lessons should be carefully noted. If it is found the teacher lacks such preparation it is time for a serious conference and a reform in her method.

7. By carefully listening to the recitation the superintendent should note whether the teacher employs good methods in questioning. The art of questioning is important in conducting a recitation. Some teachers have a way of overawing pupils to the extent that they cannot recite even what they may know. Other teachers have a way of drawing from the pupils knowledge which they did not know they possessed.

How to Assist the Teacher. Rarely should a teacher be criticised or given suggestions concerning her work before the class, since this reflects upon the teacher so that she may lose the respect of her pupils. A private conference at intermission time or after school is better. Sometimes a teacher's faults may be discussed in the teachers' meeting in a way to assist the teacher, without permitting the matter to become personal.

Occasionally a teacher lacking in method of conducting her work may receive valuable aid by visiting another room where a strong experienced teacher is in charge. Sometimes a visiting day is permitted a school to visit some neighboring school, but this plan is not to be encouraged, since it often brings criticism upon the school. If a visiting day be given, it is better that one or two teachers at a time are excused for this purpose and that they report at teachers' meeting the items they have learned from such a visit. The teacher of a school should not have the attitude of demanding a day for visiting other schools to learn methods, etc., any more than a carpenter constructing a building should require of his contractor that he be given a day to learn how to construct the building.

In the work of supervision a superintendent should seek to learn the abilities and limitations of each teacher in his school. He should have a helpful rather than a critical attitude and should not become dictatorial or autocratic in his supervision. He always should have an open mind for learning the best things and then he should be able to apply the best methods throughout his school.

Punishments. This subject legitimately may be included under the head of supervision, since many cases of discipline are brought to the office for decision and adjustment. A whole book might be written on the subject of punishments, but a few words only must suffice here.

The matter of corporal punishment must always be considered, although we hear less concerning this than formerly. In most states corporal punishment is still permitted in schools and probably sometimes this may become the best method. It is not, however, the best method with all pupils, and each case of discipline presents a problem in itself. Of course, corporal punishment should never be so severe as to endanger the health of the pupil, and it is safer if no teacher be permitted to inflict corporal punishment on a pupil unless in the presence of another teacher, the superintendent or the principal. In some schools it may be the custom for the superintendent to administer such punishment rather than the teacher. In general, however, if any punishment must be inflicted upon a pupil it should be inflicted by the one under whose authority the misdemeanor was committed. Naturally, then, a breach of rules within the school room should be attended to by the teacher in charge, while misconduct on the school ground naturally falls to the superintendent or principal of the building.

Sometimes deprivation or forfeiture of privilege is administered as a punishment, and this may be very effective. When a pupil violates a privilege it is but natural the privilege should be taken from him for a season. This is sometimes carried to such an extent, however, that the privilege of intermission is so often taken from a pupil that he looks upon the school room as a prison, and the appreciation of the school is thereby lessened. Deprivation of classroom privilege or even the school room privilege might be a better antidote for such conduct.

In general we may say that if punishment must be administered it should be such punishment as best fits the offense, and it is better if rules are not so laid that a teacher is bound to administer punishment to a pupil at any time. Punishment should not be for the purpose of injuring the pupil but rather for the reform of the pupil and the good of the school room.

An extreme mode of punishment is temporary or permanent exclusion from school. No teacher should have the power of such, and even a superintendent must consult his board of education before such punishment is meted out to any pupil, except dismissal for the day or a portion of the day.

CHAPTER X

Organizations in the School, and Social Center Activities

Recently there has been a rapid development of school organizations. This has been largely in the high schools, but the grades also have a share. The organizations have come from both an insistent demand on the part of students and pupils and a recognition by teachers of the adaptation of organizations to educational processes. The organizations probably have a legitimate place in education and in school administration, but undoubtedly schools are often over-organized, just as society is at present over-organized. Besides his regular class organization, a student has usually time for no more than one other.

Organizations are of doubtful value below the Grammar Department. Organizations to raise ideals of life and to assist in teaching good citizenship, such as the Boy Scout organization and The Camp Fire Girls' organization, are well adapted to Grammar School or Junior High School. Much of the demand for class organization comes from imitating upper classes rather than from student nature. Many school men do not encourage class organizations except the last two years of the Senior High School. The first two years of high school are better named "Ninth grade" and "Tenth grade," rather than "Freshman class" and "Sophomore class." Class organizations are by nature social, and are apt to go to extremes in a social way unless carefully held in restraint. Each class organization should have a faculty representative as counsellor and chaperone, and it is usually better that such representative be appointed by the high school principal or the superintendent rather than to be elected by the class. Class meetings should always be held in the school building and the faculty representative should attend all meetings.

Such organizations as literary societies, musical societies, athletic associations, etc., are for special purposes and should not develop into social organizations. Except the class organization, which is naturally limited to members of the class, school organizations should be democratic, allowing, as members, any students in the high school who desire to join. If an admission fee is charged, it should be placed low enough to bar no member of the school. As most states have laws prohibiting or permitting boards of education to prohibit secret organizations among high school students, it is plainly evident that these should not be tolerated in any public school.

Social Center Activities. The school's relation to the community is becoming more vital, and boards of education are demanding more and more a superintendent who takes an interest in community affairs and is willing to be a community leader in matters educational. A spirit of service for the community is also a valuable asset to a teacher. The following are suggestive items in making the school a community factor and the school building a community center:

(a) The superintendent should always make his home in the community which he serves, and he will do well to take an active interest, so far as his regular school duties will permit, in the legitimate activities of the community.

(b) Teachers should room and board in the community, at least during the school week. They should likewise have an active interest in community welfare. The practice by some teachers of leaving the community every Friday evening and returning the following Monday morning is usually detrimental to the strength of the teacher in the community.

(c) Teachers will enhance their worth and the appreciation of the community if they visit the homes of their pupils and interest the parents in the school work.

(d) The school should be made a community center. The following are suggestive ways:

1. By occasionally having a "go-to-school day" for patrons.

2. By having an annual exhibit day and evening, for the public, and through the pupils have personal invitations sent. Music may be furnished, lunches served, or other means used as special attraction.

3. By occasionally giving public evening programs by pupils and teachers. In some communities schools successfully maintain a public evening lecture course, or a winter chautauqua course.

4. By having pupils, rooms or classes appear upon the program of community gatherings, or assist in parades, etc., on special occasions.

5. By public school athletic, musical or literary contests.

6. By organizing and maintaining a parent-teacher association.

7. By annual presentation of a class or school play.

8. By public graduating exercises. These are more effective if given without admission fee.

9. By placing the school building at the disposal of patrons for legitimate public gatherings.

10. By using the building for social gatherings of the students, always under direct supervision of the superintendent.

With the demand for the school as a community center and as a live educational factor in the community, there has also been brought forward the idea of extension service by the school throughout the district, much as state colleges carry extension work to communities throughout the state. By means of federal, state and local aid, night schools are being established in some cities to carry the work of the school to the adult population. Part-time schools are also being established to reach children of school age who for some reason left school before completing the course. Home Economics departments are serving hot lunches to pupils and giving demonstrations for the benefit of mothers and laboring girls. Agriculture classes are testing seeds for farmers and testing milk from individual cows, etc. All this makes added responsibility for those responsible for the school, but it also renders the school a more vital factor in the community and makes the citizens of the community more appreciative of the school.

CHAPTER XI

Putting Over a Building Campaign

General Statement. It is the unusual experience of a superintendent, who, at least once in his career, does not have the experience of conducting a campaign for a new school building, and some superintendents go through a building campaign several times. School board members also have a large part in conducting such campaigns in a district. While every district has its distinct problem in the success of such a campaign, a few general principles which apply to all may be stated.

Preparing the Way. Bonds for a new building must be submitted to the qualified voters of the district for approval, and a majority of votes cast must be favorable to the issue if the bond issue be carried. The submission of the question must be done by the Board of Education. Preliminary steps are necessary. First of all the community must be informed of the need and educated to the advantage to be gained by providing a new building, whether the new building be provided as an additional building or to replace an old, inadequate building. It is better if the information be given some time in advance, and not sprung upon the community just previous to the vote. The need should, of course, be real and not imaginary. The community should be taken into confidence, and no exaggerated statements of the need be permitted.

Method of Procedure. The superintendent and the Board of Education should discuss at length and in advance the size and type of building needed, the approximate cost, the proper location and the time for the vote on the proposition. The bonded indebtedness of the district at the time should be taken into account in making the estimate, as well as the legal limitations of the district. A survey should be made of the probable future needs of the district. If the district does not have a regular attorney a legal advisor should be provided, so that no false steps will invalidate the action.

Some districts employ an architect to draw up tentative plans for the proposed building, and a cut is secured in advance and used in the local press. This gives reality to the project and interests the voters. A large sketch may be prepared and exhibited in a store window or in some other conspicuous place. Usually an architect will do the preliminary work of this kind without requiring compensation, in case the vote is not favorable to the proposition. He is willing to take this chance in order to secure the work as architect in case the issue is successful. Another plan is to leave the choosing of an architect and plans for the building until the election has been held and the issue favorably decided.

Choosing an Architect. This is rather an important matter. In either of the above plans an architect may be chosen somewhat competitively, by allowing several architects to interview the "Board." Each architect presents a plan for the proposed building. The terms of the architect, the proposed type of building and especially his reputation should be taken into account. Not only a general reputation as architect, but a reputation especially as an architect for school buildings should be considered. It may be possible in some instances for members of the Board of Education to see school buildings already erected by certain architects. Arthitects, in general, charge the same percentage rate as fee in constructing a building, but some architects present two plans, one for complete supervision of the work and one for local supervision by a competent person chosen by the Board of Education.

In regard to the employment of an architect one caution ought to be suggested. Occasionally an architect has a certain type of building he prefers to erect, and he attempts to force this style of building on each local district by which he may be employed. Local conditions differ and such type of building may not be desirable for certain districts. Boards of education should have minds of their own regarding the type of building needed. It is a wise plan in advance for the superintendent and all members of the Board of Education to visit some neighboring modern school buildings and ascertain the type of building best suited to the local needs.

The Campaign. When it is finally decided by the Board of Education that the issue shall be placed before the people of the district, the amount of bonds to call for and the general plan of building desired are important matters to consider. The time to set for the vote to be taken is important. If indications are that the vote will be close and the result doubtful, these matters become the more important. Often the vote on the issue is taken at the annual meeting for the election of new board members. This has the advantage of capitalizing on the natural interest in the election to secure a large vote. On the other hand the contest on certain candidates may defeat the proposition. The opposition may place as candidate a popular citizen opposed to the building project, and he may carry with him votes enough to defeat the proposition. In such case it would be better to vote on the issue at another time and make it a separate issue.

Legally a vote on a bond issue must be advertised a certain number of weeks in advance. This period should be used as a period of publicity and of education of the community to the school needs. The following are suggestive ways:

(a) Use local press. Editors are usually in sympathy with a progressive movement for the schools. Short statements by leading citizens, both men and women, may be published from week to week.

(b) Local pastors may be induced to present the matter to their congregations or allow some spokesman chosen by the school to present the matter to the congregation.

(c) A mass meeting may be held and an outside speaker of prominence secured to give an address on the subject of "Better Schools." This meeting should be open to questions or discussion by any citizen.

(d) Local organizations may be asked to send one or more representatives to the school to investigate conditions and report their findings to such organization.

(e) A publicity committee of citizens may be chosen by the local "Board" to study the needs and present them to the public.

(f) Occasionally students may be utilized by parades, etc., but this method is questionable, as it may react on the promoters of the building plan.

(g) The town may be districted and a responsible person chosen in each district to agitate the matter in such district and interest the voters.

(h) Automobiles and other conveyances may be used to bring voters to the polls.

(i) A circular of information may be issued and circulated in the community.

In all this the main thing is to secure the interest of the voters in the project and to secure a maximum vote. Usually the opposition to a proposition of this kind is organized and the opposition force will poll a maximum vote. This is not always true of the proponents of the measure, and some voters really in favor of the project are apt, through partial indifference or a feeling that the measure will carry anyway, to remain away from the polls. The campaign should be placed on a high plane and the endeavor should be to secure a maximum vote of the district, so as to obtain a real public expression on the question. If conveyances are offered to convey voters to the polls who otherwise could not well go, the offer should be made to all voters, regardless of whether the vote is to be affirmative or negative.

After the Battle. Of course, a campaign of this kind is not always a battle, although there is usually some organized opposition to bonding the district for a school plant. No matter how mild nor how fierce the contest may have been, when it is over there should be no display of bonfires, parades,. etc., to celebrate victory. This is apt to leave an unnecessary bitter feeling. The great American principle of "fair play" and the "rule of the majority" should prevail. If the issue is lost, no bitter criticism should be used, but a steady campaign of education may go on so that the matter may be presented again at a later time. If the issue wins, the responsibility of the Board of Education is to prepare, through the architect, complete plans for the building and advertise for bids by contractors. Matters should be pushed along as rapidly as consistent with material plans. The mistake should not be made of promising to the district a new building by a certain date, for such promise can rarely be fulfilled and this leaves disappointment and criticism.

CHAPTER XII

The Teacher and Her Work

Importance of the Teacher. Without the teacher there could be no school. No matter how excellent the school plant, how complete the equipment, or how nearly perfect the course of study, these could not function in education without the live teacher to connect it all with the living pupil. Someone has estimated that the teacher constitutes 85 per cent of the efficiency of the school. It is of course impossible to evaluate the service of the teacher numerically, but educators and laymen alike will agree that a competent and willing teacher is the largest single factor in bringing education to the child.

Her Attitude. The calling of the teacher is perhaps the most unfortunate from one standpoint of all the professions. Those found in the work of medicine, law or the ministry are usually there because they feel either a strong liking for the work, adaptability to it, or both combined. They are also in the profession with the intention of making such profession a life work and a life study. This is not true to the same extent in the profession of teaching. Some there be, it is true, who have a natural love for the work, a conceived adaptability to it, and who enter the profession with the intention of making teaching a life pursuit. This number, however, constitutes the small minority of teachers.

This fact shapes to a large extent the attitude of the teacher. Many teachers go into the work as a temporary expedient, and because of the large number of teachers demanded, this will probably always be true. Indeed, this fact may not be an unmitigated evil. Because of it, there are bright, keen young men and women who spend a few years of their young, enthusiastic, energetic and optimistic lives as teachers of youth, and bring thus to the schools hope, vigor and enthusiasm that is worth while. They are often of the highly ambitious type; many of our adult social, business and political leaders of today have taught school some time, and they often express a longing for the schoolroom again.

Preparation. While this is true it does mean that teachers are temporarily drawn into schoolroom work without proper preparation for it. The position is a stepping stone to some other work or career, hence not enough time and attention is given to scientific preparation for teaching. This is unfortunate for the schools. Those getting higher education in preparation for another profession may often teach some, to pay for their education or to get a little ready money in advance to tide over the "starving period" of such a calling. This may be a fine experience for the young man or the young woman, but it is far from being satisfactory to the pupils. There is no calling more in need of careful preparation and thorough training than the calling involving the health, the intellect and the spiritual emotions of boys and girls. Developing boys and girls change rapidly and are complex in their structure. A teacher should understand all phases of child life and should be trained in methods of dealing with the child.

The only possible cure for this condition is for the schools to demand properly educated and properly trained teachers. Teachers in any department of the school should not only be educated in subject matter, but should be thoroughly trained in methods of teaching boys and girls.

Normal schools and educational departments in colleges and universities now provide such instruction and training for teachers. It only remains for schools exclusively to employ trained teachers. The objection may be raised that the expense is too great. If a school system has all well qualified teachers, these teachers can accomplish far more than can untrained teachers. Trained teachers are therefore cheaper teachers.

Special Training. Schools, like other institutions, are to some extent becoming a field for specialists. This has not as yet, however, developed to any alarming extent. Boys and girls have the same mind and the same temperament whether they are studying Music or studying Arithmetic. The specialty of the teacher, therefore, consists rather in the special knowledge of the subject to be taught than in the special method of teaching the subject. Of course the varying ages of children have considerable to do with methods of teaching. A well trained Primary teacher could not be expected to do as well teaching High School boys and girls. There is no reason, however, why a trained Primary teacher may not be able to teach any of the three Primary grades. Neither is there any reason why a Grammar room teacher may not succeed with Intermediate pupils, nor why a High School teacher may not be able to teach Grammar School pupils.

Since correlation is so important a factor in school work there is some danger in over-specialization. When a teacher pleads that she can teach but a certain grade or a certain subject, suspicion may well be aroused as to the value of such teacher.

This should not be understood as advocating no special training, as such has an important place. Much of such specialization, though, is rather in imagination than in fact. Because a high school teacher in her preparation has majored in mathematics is no reason why she may not teach some History, nor because another teacher is interested particularly in the works of the great literary composers is it proof that she must be given only third and fourth year English and no Rhetoric work to teach.

A Fallacy.   There is one very harmful and mistaken idea often held by boards of education, superintendents and teachers.   This is to the effect that for high school we must have thoroughly prepared teachers, college graduates, but for grade work a meager preparation is sufficient.   In such thinking we fail to recognize that the child mind is just as much a problem as the mind of youth.   Indeed, the pre-adolescent mind of grammar school pupils is most complicated.   In the lower grades pupils need more direction and help than in the high school, and here, too, it is doubly important that right habits of work and study be fixed.   High School students are able to direct their own efforts largely, but this is not true of lower grade pupils.   ·Grade teachers may possibly not need so much training in the college informational subjects, but they certainly need as much knowledge and training in "Education" and in pedagogical methods.   There is too much difference in the size of the pay envelopes of the grade teacher and the high school teacher.   Often there are found young, inexperienced teachers in high school, just out of college and with no previous teaching experience, drawing a much larger salary than a trained, experienced grade teacher in the same school.   Such teacher may be entitled to some consideration for her extra one or two years of college work, but the disparity in remuneration is **too** great.   Several factors enter into the matter of salary schedule, and scholarship is but one of these factors.

Factors of Success. Some teachers fail, others succeed, while still others become but mediocre in their work. This sometimes happens even when preparation for the work is on a par. It is difficult often to account for the difference, but some factors may be ascertained. The degree of success of a teacher is often fixed the first year of her teaching. Her environment may help to make or to mar her record. No doubt it is a great help to a teacher the first year of her experience to work with a helpful superintendent, one who will assist her in solving her problems. Here is an excellent opportunity to receive training in service. The attitude of the teacher, on the other hand, may be such as to refuse proffered help. Again a teacher may be helped by associating with other successful teachers in the school.

A teacher sometimes fails through lack of strong initiative in her work. She rests upon what she has learned in her training school and expects such methods learned to solve all her problms. Again she may fail because of lack of daily preparation in lessons; indeed this is considered a prolific cause of failure.

Some teachers fail of full success because of lack of the spirit of co-operation with pupils, parents, teachers or the superintendent. A spirit of jealousy prevents the necessary friendly spirit. Lack of sympathy for certain pupils and partiality toward others often enter in, to a teacher's detriment. A teacher should zealously cultivate a spirit of fairmindedness. No matter how we feel about it, common sense should make us realize that the parent is a factor in the education of the child and that he is more intensely interested in the child than the teacher can be. A parent should therefore be treated courteously and with open mind.

Attitude Toward School Officials and the Community. It goes without saying that a teacher should treat school officials with consideration and respect. They are always entitled to this, and teachers generally so treat them. Sometimes, on the other hand, there is not shown the co-operative spirit that is due. The teacher is one factor in the school, the school official is another. For best service these two factors must harmonize.

The community, the patrons of the school, are entitled not only to respect and co-operation, but solicitous consideration from teachers. They are the ones most interested in the children's welfare and the ones who sacrifice most that they may receive an education. Sometimes a teacher in a certain instance is provoked into the thought that the parent does not care whether the child learns anything or not. There may be such cases, but they are indeed rare. Parents do not always understand the school, its purpose, its methods or the acts of the teacher, and for this reason they may give uuwarranted criticism. Teachers may rest assured, however, that they have interest in the progress of their children in the school.

For the above reason it is important that early in the year the teacher get acquainted with the parents of her pupils. In this way much trouble may be avoided and better co-operation exist. A few parents will come to the teacher for this acquaintance, but in most cases the teacher must go to the parents, for many fathers and mothers are too diffident and have a feeling that they would not be welcome at the school.

It is a deplorable fact that there is coming to be a feeling these later days among some groups of teachers that a teacher's task is assigning lessons, hearing recitations and disciplining the pupils, and as soon as the scheduled school day comes to a close the work of the teacher is done for that day and that her time is her own until the next day at 8:30 or 9:00 o'clock A. M. While a teacher should take some time each day for relaxation, recreation and personal enjoyment, if she be "true blue" she cannot teach school by the clock. A child may need assistance before school or after school to the extent that involves his failure or success in the grade and in his future career. Shall a teacher deny such help? A physieian or a minister could as well refuse assistance to patient or parishioner after office or study hours. If teaching is to be a profession it should, like other professions, be put on the basis of service instead of on the basis of maximum hours per day. Any teacher who cannot subscribe to the doctrine of service should leave the profession. The welfare of children is too sacred a trust to be placed in the hands of a mercenary.

Much of this chapter may seem to be in criticism of our great body of teachers in the public schools. The author does not intend it so, for he has the highest regard for that great body of loyal teachers who are conscientiously serving the district in which they are employed and who daily by kind ministration seek to make the way smoother for the neglected and unfortunate children under their charge. The criticism is only for that small minority of teachers who have not yet caught the vision of true service. Rest assured these will learn better or fall by the wayside, for school officials in these days of expensive education are more and more going to demand of teachers, principals and superintendents both efficiency and service. This ought to be a good omen for the true servant of the schools, for she will then get her full recognition.

A Noble Calling. Teachers sometimes may seem to be unappreciated. It is mostly in the "seeming." There is a general recognition of the fact that the teacher stands next to the parent in importance to the child. She assists in a large and important measure in molding and shaping the future of the children placed in her charge. If she be a real teacher it may truly be said of her that "The future generation shall arise to call her 'blessed.'" To an experienced teacher there often comes a former pupil with an expression of appreciation for being patiently helped over the hard places.

The teacher is an important part of the school system, and will always be such. While she has not always been recognized at her true value in the way of salary schedule, there are evidences that she is receiving fairer compensation now than ever before, and that the true, prepared and efficient teacher will continue to receive more adequate salary. Many states are also providing annuities for teachers long in the service, so the profession of teaching is being placed on a more stable basis. There's a better day ahead.

CHAPTER XIII

The Board of Education

In another chapter the functions of the Board of Education have been discussed. The subject of the "Board" itself, however, merits further discussion, since the members of the "Board" are the persons who really make possible the school. The Board of Education is the intermediary between tax payers and the pupils. Through the activities of the "Board" the school is made to function.

Who May Be Members. Of course any qualified voter in the district who receives an election or an appointment as such may serve as member of the Board of Education. This does not indicate, however, that every voter is qualified to render good service in that capacity. The service calls for both ability and spirit of service. Good business ability and a comprehension of educational problems are needed to render good service here. This does not mean that board members shall be experienced in educational work nor that they be highly educated men. They should realize the needs and the possibilities of good schools, and these they may realize by the limitations in their own education.

Sometimes a superintendent will boast that the Board of Education in his district consists entirely of college graduates. No doubt it is a decided advantage if one or more members of the "Board" be highly educated, for thus will all other members have leadership in educational policies. Professional men therefore usually make good "Board" members. What is needed just as much, however, is ability and experience in business, and good business men should also be sought for service in this capacity.   School is a business, and should have behind it sound business policies.   Business ability is not necessarily, either, confined to that gained in commercial enterprises.   Business ability may be gained through leadership in organization work or the successful handling of large problems in any way.   The two qualifications, business and educational, represented on a Board of Education, whether both qualities are found in the same person or in different members, make a splendid combination.

It was formerly considered irrelevant to elect as member of a Board of Education any man who did not himself have children in school.   Education now, however, has become of such general interest that this distinction need not obtain.   Ten years ago, also, "Board" members were almost exclusively composed of men.   Today an increasing unmber of women are being elected to the position.   There is no good reason why women may not become valuable "Board" members, although certain school problems are of such a nature that it would seem there should always be a majority of men as members.

In some communities there is difficulty in inducing competent men to become members of the Board of Education, either through fear of mistakes and criticism which might injure such men's business, or because their own business engrosses their whole time and attention, so that they feel they cannot spare the time.   This is most unfortunate, since it then leaves this responsible position to mediocre ability, to men who seek the place for the honor involved in the position; or sometimes even worse, to men who desire the position to enhance their own political schemes.   There is no official position in any community which should more demand the efficient and the patriotic service of its best citizens than a position which so closely touches and molds the lives of all the children of the community.

Shall "Board" Members Be Compensated for Service? Sometimes we hear criticism that men and women who give valuable time and spend precious energy thus for the schools should not be paid for such service. It is generally considered, on the other hand, that the schools get a higher type of service because of its gratuitous nature. The position in most districts could not command enough compensation to interest the best ability, and politics would prevail much more in the election or appointment of members. As it is, men and women do not seek the position for compensation, but usually accept it through interest in the cause of education or as an opportunity to serve the community.

In every community an appeal should be made to the competent men and women to accept, in their turn, a term or two as members of the Board of Education. The author served as superintendent in one district where the members of the local Chamber of Commerce had a mutual understanding that they would take their turns as they were called upon to serve the city or the schools in an official capacity for a term or two, and would not refuse such duty when asked to become candidates for election. They were willing to do this as a civic duty.

It would be well if a law might be passed, however, permitting expenses and per diem to be paid all board members, or at least a representative from each board in the state to a conference once per year to be called by county or state officials. This would enable members of the "Board," without financial loss to themselves, to meet with like officials from other schools for discussion of mutual problems, and to receive instruction concerning their duties. It would also make possible a unity of purpose and program among the various Boards of Education in the state.

Organization of the "Board." Mention has been made briefly in a previous chapter concerning the organization work. Two things seem important, one to avoid too much machinery in the organization. In large city districts, of course, the work must be complex, but in the average district it may and should be simple. A few committees should be appointed, but the vital problems should be settled by the "Board" as a whole. Special committees may be appointed as occasion demands, for investigations, and the results of such investigations, with recommendations, should be brought before the whole "Board" for determination. The other important consideration is that there should be held regular periodic meetings of the "Board" to pass on bills against the district and to consider business matters in connection with the schools. Such meetings are usually held in the evening, although they may be held at any time most convenient to all members. During the school year the meetings should be held at a time when the superintendent may be present, as the best interests of the schools are served when board members and superintendent confer together. In most districts the regular meetings should be held once per month, and in larger districts perhaps more often. Of course a special meeting may be called at any time.

Occasionally there is found in a district what is known as a "one-man board." One member of the board, with more experience in school matters, with more education, with more time at his disposal or with some personal persuasion some way assumes most of the direction of school affairs. No doubt this is more often because of neglect by other members in assuming their share of responsibility than by assumption of authority on his part. In either case, however, it makes a bad situation. It is a clear case of "two heads are better than one." In carrying out the decisions of the "Board," such may well be placed in one man's hands, but in making those decisions all members should have a part. We should remember that the Board of Education is primarily a legislative body, not an executive head, so all important matters should be determined by all members. The body is small enough so that this may well be done.

Legal Advice. Because the duties of a Board of Education often involve legal matters some "Boards" employ an attorney by the year, that is, retain his services as occasion requires, compensating him for such service as he may render. If this cannot be done the county attorney may be consulted on occasion. Usually the county superintendent is well versed in school laws and will be glad to give advice. The State Department of Instruction on request is always glad to give advice on legal matters.

A "Board" will do well at all times to keep in touch with county and state school officials. Valuable literature may be secured from this source and standards the more easily maintained. School officials are for the service of schools and usually welcome opportunities to assist in this way.

Suggested Co-operative Plan. From several sources there have come a request and a demand for reorganization of school control. Such school people believe that teachers themselves, or through their committee, should have some voice in direct administration of the school, even to passing upon recommendations of teachers, etc. They somehow resent the power that a superintendent may have. Some even advocate the representation of the teachers on the Board of Education, since they feel that teachers are in position to know the needs of the school better than members of the community not in so close touch with the work of the school.

These advocates are no doubt sincere in their endeavor to better the work of the schools, but they lose sight of two fundamental facts:

1. The school is a community enterprise, provided, maintained and financed by the patrons of the district, not by the teachers. The teachers, principals and superintendent are employes of the district. If they are also residents of and voters in the district they are already represented on the "Board" as truly as any other citizens; if not residents, they are not entitled to such representation.

2. That a school, the same as any other business, must have a responsible head, and not a committee to handle executive affairs. Even our municipal affairs are now rapidly being placed under single administrative control through appointment of a city manager as executive head.

A progressive and wise superintendent is always ready to seek advice from his teachers, and no doubt he can receive valuable help from them in solving internal problems of school planning. They are more in touch with details of student problems. The Board of Education also may secure valuable advice from teachers at times. Many large schools have teacher organizations and the "Board" as well as the superintendent may secure valuable co-operation from such organizations. The main control of the school, however, should be by one executive head, an educated and experienced superintendent, chosen by the representatives of the district, the Board of Education.

Status and Tenure of a Superintendent. In many states the legal duties of a superintendent are not defined or are very meagerly defined. In such cases each district may be a unit in establishing the status of the superintendent. This is unfortunate, as there should be some general plan followed by all districts within the state. A state law fixing the status of a superintendent of schools and defining his rights and duties would be welcomed generally by both superintendents and school officials. Heretofore school boards have had no conferences with other boards, to arrive at a general procedure, but in some states organizations of board members are being formed to work out mutual problems of this kind. Each local board may, however, and should work out a definite plan, or rules, showing where the jurisdiction of the "Board" ends and that of the superintendent begins. This would often prevent embarrassment to both parties. Two matters in particular should be included in such plan, first that individual "Board" members should not listen to complaints against the school, but that complainants should appear before the whole "Board" in session; second, that the superintendent should in general be elected before the teachers are elected, and that he should have the privilege of recommending teachers for election. This does not mean that the "Board" is bound to elect everyone recommended, but it should mean that no teacher be elected to whom the superintendent seriously objects. The superintendent is the one most responsible for the success of the school, so it is only fair that he shall have a corps of teachers who will work in harmony with him. The nature of his training and experience renders his judgment better in selection of teachers for the various positions in the school.

In selection of a superintendent for a system of schools it is becoming increasingly evident that there should not be frequent changes in this position. This finds expression in laws in some states permitting a superintendent to be employed for three or more years in advance. Where this is permitted, the custom of such extended employment is gaining ground. It is evident that even in a small school system a year is too short a time for a superintendent to work out a definite program or to make a strong impress upon the school or the community. Another growing practice is to elect a superintendent for the full year of twelve months instead of for the school year of nine months. Since the school is becoming a community center and the superintendent a community leader, the reason is plain. There are many interests of the school which need attention during the vacation months. Since it is difficult for the superintendent to find, during this short period, other remunerative work, it does not cost a district much more to engage him for the full year.

The School Year. The school today has a more crowded curriculum than formerly. This has led to scattered experiments in extending the school year from nine months to practically the calendar year, or to forty-eight weeks. Usually in such cases the summer months have been given over to backward pupils and to others electing to take the work, and the attendance has not been made compulsory. The increased cost of school maintenance the past few years has served temporarily to check such experimentation. On the other hand, in some districts there is an unfortunate tendency to shorten the school day by lengthening the noon intermission period and closing earlier than four o'clock in the afternoon. Possibly in some instances this may be justifiable, but with the crowded curriculum it would seem to be more logical to lengthen the school day for older pupils. This would enable the pupils to prepare more of their work under school supervision, and would assist in solving the difficult problem of home study.

At present there are many demands made upon the schools for closing school a day or two at a time. Some of these are legitimate, of course, and some are legally required. "Boards" are sometimes puzzled to know where to draw the line. There is no question, of course, concerning the days schools are legally required to be closed. In different states legal holidays are considered variously. In a few, schools are legally required to be closed, in others the matter is optional in each district. Certain holidays, of course, should be observed, such as Thanksgiving, Christmas and Memorial Day, since these are patriotic days or days of national significance. Unless legally required or unless the community celebrates the occasion, there seems to be no good reason why school should be closed such days as Washington's birthday or Lincoln's birthday. Usually such days can be observed more appropriately with schools in session and by means of some appropriate exercises in each department. If local sentiment or tradition dictates the closing of school such days, however, the school may appropriately prepare a community program for afternoon or evening.

Teachers' institutes, conventions, etc., claim some legitimate and legal rights for closing school, of course. Within reasonable limits such are worth while, as teachers get valuable help from these meetings. Except as to legal requirements, however, there is as yet no settled policy in these matters. The closing of school is optional with the "Board," and the question as to whether teachers in attendance at the convention will receive instruction and inspiration which will make them better teachers in the school, is important to consider. The request for one or two days per year for teachers to visit other schools, however, is different. Closing school for such purposes is not customary nor prevalent, and is of doubtful value.

Owing to the numerous unavoidable occasions when school must be closed for a day or two, a few districts have extended the school year to nine and one-half months, the last week being given over largely to examinations, school exercises, reports, etc.

Financial Limitations. Each state legally requires (with certain exceptions), that every school district shall maintain each year a minimum number of months of school. It also fixes a maximum amount that may be levied in any year for school purposes. Between these two extremes there is considerable range.

It is no doubt unnecessary to caution against either penury or extravagance in financing schools, for it is not presumable that any school officials purposely handle school matters either way. Yet it is true that we find some schools crippled in their work because of poor or inadequate equipment, by employment of cheap and inferior teachers, etc. On the other hand a school sometimes spends so much for an elaborate school plant or for a profusion of costly equipment that the school is driven to economize for a number of years on proper maintenance of the school. Either plan shows lack of careful thought on the part of officials. Perhaps some inexperienced superintendent in his zeal may recommend for a moderate sized school things that only larger systems may afford. One mistake small or moderate sized schools sometimes make is to try to emulate larger school systems in school plant, elaborate equipment or varied curriculum. The small school system involves largely a different problem than a large school system.

In employment of qualified and experienced teachers, however, the small school system may and should be just as ambitious as the larger school system. Strong teachers are needed here just as much as in the larger school; the interests of the children are just as sacred. If eighty-five per cent of the efficiency of the school is due to the teachers, then it is wise economy to secure the best teachers available. While the small district does not have the large property valuation of the large district, neither does it have so many teachers to employ. In fact the school levy in mills is usually larger in the cities than in the smaller centers. There is no evident reason why, in order to maintain an effective school, the smaller school may not bear as large a levy in mills as the large district. Except in the matter of diversity of high school courses, the smaller district may thus maintain just as good a school as the larger district, except where the district is so small that there are not pupils enough for fair-sized classes.

Suggestions for Providing and Care of Equipment. Providing of equipment is necessarily somewhat expensive, and some schools are therefore limited in amount that may be provided in a given year. In such cases the most important articles should be first procured and other articles purchased the following year. In this way the expense can be equalized. Because equipment is expensive, care should be taken that it be used as intended and properly protected from injury when not in use. The following are a few suggestions in procuring various kinds of equipment:

1. Deal only with reliable firms.
2. Secure only standard articles.
3. Order early enough to avoid delay in receiving articles. Orders for use the first of the school year should be placed six months earlier, so as to allow firms to handle the orders well.

4. Always check carefully and promptly all articles received, and at once notify firms of shortages or errors in shipment.

5. In purchase of tools, etc., the "make" should be considered.

6. In purchase of maps, charts and books, authorship is important; accuracy should be considered, as well as date of publication.

7. Maps and charts are better if hand-mounted on double muslin.

8. Maps should be of suitable size for use in the ordinary class-room and should be such that they may be easily moved from room to room.

9. Textbooks in use should be occasionally changed, a few at a time, for more modern, up-to-date texts.

10. In purchase of dictionary, atlas or encyclopedia, authorship, size of volumes, type, number of volumes, binding, date of publication and general construction should be considered.

11. Much playground equipment of simple nature, such as swings, turning poles, teeter-boards and giant strides may be made locally, in the Manual Training rooms.

12. In purchase of equipment in large quantities a saving may sometimes be made by getting quotations from several firms.

In proper care of all kinds of equipment the following suggestions are in place:

1. In each room or department a careful inventory should be taken both at beginning and close of school year.

2. Proper racks, shelves or cases for storing articles when not in use should be provided. Books and science equipment should be in dry room and dust-proof cases.

3. Cases should be properly stored and locked in vacation time.

4. The teacher should have definite responsibility over use of equipment in her room or department, and should be held responsible for unnecessary loss or breakage.

5. Each pupil should be made to feel individual responsibility in handling equipment, and may even be asked to replace articles carelessly broken or lost by him.

6. All articles should be kept clean and in good order. Tools should be kept sharp.

7. Each teacher should have a list of articles to be used by her room or department and know where to find such easily.

8. The superintendent should have general oversight of all equipment and should supervise its care and use.

9. The superintendent should ask a report once or twice per year from each teacher in regard to use and care of equipment.

10. The Board of Education may well require an annual report from the superintendent in the same way at the close of the school year.

Problems to Consider. The school is a growing institution, and new problems constantly arise. A school that is adequate for one generation or even one decade will prove to be inadequate for the next. Although some critics may exclaim to the contrary, the schools are now more efficient on the whole than they have ever been before. If space would permit, proofs might be brought to justify this statement.

There are several evident deficiencies in our school system today which were not so conspicuous a decade ago. These are now receiving serious consideration in every state by both educators and school officials. No attempt is here made to point the way to their solution, but merely to call attention to the most important problems.

1. There is a feeling, first of all, that school work should be more vitalized, or motivated. It is seen that much of the work does not properly function in the daily lives of pupils.

2. There is not the proper balance between the so-called "cultural" subjects and the vocational subjects, or rather these two types of work are not being properly correlated.

3. The school work is over-intellectualized, that is, we are emphasizing fact material and mental training to the exclusion of physical and moral training.

4. Citizenship training, or the teaching of patriotism, has not received sufficient attention.

5. Vocational training should be coupled some way with vocational guidance, so that the students may more easily find their true calling, or occupation in life.

6. Proper sex hygiene should in some way receive attention by or through the schools.

7. We should teach boys and girls how to properly use their leisure as well as to guide them into their vocation.

8. We should more thoroughly democratize our school work, that is, fit it more for use of the masses of children. More efficient compulsory school laws would assist in this.

9. A proper way needs to be developed to decrease retardation of pupils, both those above normal ability as well as those below normal. This resolves itself into a need for reclassification of pupils according to ability instead of according to age.

The above are the more important problems now being considered. Attempts are being made to solve these and already some are on the way to evident solution. In some of these the larger schools, those possessing better facilities, must lead the way. Others may be solved by the smaller schools, as well as by the larger system.

Recognition of Service. Since the office of member of a board of education is of a gratuitous nature, and since it involves both sacrifice of time and energy, a community should certainly appreciate the honest efforts in such service. While "Board" members are sometimes criti-cised for their official acts, the same as all public servants, there are evidences that the public in general does appre-ciate such service. The compensation comes through enriched experience, through increased interest in child welfare, and in a feeling of service rendered. The author knows one ex-"Board" member, a busy professional man. who now rejoices that for seventeen years in succession he assisted officially in building up a system of schools, nine of those years as President of the Board of Educa-tion. Through this service he extended his acquaintance from his clientele to the whole community, gained some lasting friends, received the respect of the student body and enlarged his knowledge of local, state and national educational affairs. This is to him a rich legacy in his later years. Someone has said that "The sweetest serv-ice we render is that for which we are not paid." The service of a school official, if rendered through honest effort, although possibly fraught with many errors, is a noble service. Such officials have the deep-rooted respect of the community, and this respect is enduring. Is it not therefore worth the sacrifice of time and energy, es-pecially when it is realized that the service rendered helps the boys and girls of the community?

CHAPTER XIV

General Consideration

Before concluding this subject a few miscellaneous matters should claim our attention, matters of a general nature which do not group themselves readily under the preceding chapters.

Tenure of Office. A superintendent is often puzzled to know how long he shall stay in one position. Of course, if he is not successful or is unsatisfactory to the community he does not need to decide that point; it will be decided for him. If he is giving satisfaction, however, which is more often the case, he is especially ambitious for a large school system, looking for "More worlds to conquer". This is a worthy ambition, but is apt to lead the young superintendent to too frequent changes in position and to the habit of not seeing through a program he outlines in a school. It is safe to say that no constructive program of merit can show results in one year. The plan of changing schools each year is bad for the school and just as bad for the superintendent. The tenure of the position depends, of course, on the size of the school system, the larger school system requiring more time to carry through a program than the smaller system. In the small system of schools, employing from six to ten teachers, the good of the school, as well as the future good of the superintendent would seem to require a tenure of three to five years, in a larger system a somewhat longer tenure. Of course a longer tenure is better for the school.

Shall a Superintendent Instruct, and in What Branches? In a small system of schools it is usually necessary that a superintendent teach several subjects. He cannot always choose the subjects he shall teach, for sometimes he must take charge of those subjects for which no other teachers are prepared. In the final analysis this is often a benefit to the superintendent, although it may not always be best for the classes. Many experienced superintendents claim that the teaching of the various subjects in their early career has enabled them better to keep in touch with and supervise the high school work later. Owing to the many demands on the time of a superintendent, it is usually better for him to teach subjects without laboratory periods and without many papers to examine. Many superintendents of large school systems prefer to teach one or two subjects in the high school, in order that they may thus become better acquainted with the student body. Some also select Ninth grade subjects so they may become acquainted with students as soon as they enter high school.

Oral Work vs. Written Work. The relative value of oral work and written work sometimes comes in for consideration. Some teachers favor much written work, making of booklets, writing of compositions, etc. This gives definiteness to the work and gives the teacher concrete evidence of the quality and quantity of the pupil's work. It should not be wholly depended upon, however, as the pupil may have received help in preparing it. Much oral work should balance this as a test of the pupil's ability and preparation. Again, oral work has a value of its own in training in expression and development of confidence. English teachers are turning more to oral work. Part of the Spelling work, no doubt, should be oral, for best results. Much oral demonstration work is valuable. The two forms of work should be well balanced in every year of the school.

Methods of Promotion. In general, the elementary pupils are promoted by grades; that is, when all the subjects are completed, at a certain minimum percentage, in a certain grade, the pupil is entitled to enter the next grade. This is by yearly promotions in the smaller school system. If a pupil fails of reaching the minimum percentage in but one subject, he must repeat the whole year's work. This is a discouragement to the pupil, creates a group of "retarded pupils" in each grade and adds to the expenditure of maintaining the school. To remedy this, some schools now base promotions on the successful completion of only certain major subjects in each grade; others base it on a successful percentage of a certain proportion of the subjects, for instance, four subjects of the five studied or five of the six studied. Many schools base promotions in the Primary department on general fitness rather than on percentages. Many superintendents promote a pupil every second year whether he can "make his grade," or not. This is on the assumption that it is better for both pupil and the school that the pupil be kept with other pupils somewhat near his age. There is a growing tendency to base promotion on individual merit, and to promote a pupil any time during the year that he is thought capable of doing the next grade work. In the high school the promotion matter is simple, as each student is given credit for a year's work or a half year's work in a given subject. Seventy-five per cent is the usual passing mark in both grades and high school.

Intelligence tests are used in some schools as a basis for promoting "retarded" pupils and exceptionally precocious pupils. The method of applying of this test should be thoroughly understood before being used.

The Place of Special Tests. In recent years many schools have been using special speed, accuracy and ability tests prepared for such purposes by experts in the field of education.   These are valuable and comparatively easy to handle.   They are an incentive to the pupils, a spur to the teacher and constitute a plan to compare results with those of other school systems.   The direct educational value of such tests is not so great as the indirect value.   They should not be allowed, therefore, to consume too much time of the school.

School Surveys.   These are rather for the larger system of schools and are elaborate in nature.   For the small system they are impractical.   However, the superintendent of a small school can receive value by studying the report of the survey of some city system.   He can get therefrom the relative expenditure of different factors of the school.   He can thus make a survey of his own system and compare results.   The value of any survey is to detect waste, extravagance and inefficiency that may exist in some departments of the school.

What a Superintendent Should Know About His School and Community.   Often gross ignorance is found on the part of a superintendent regarding important matters.   In such cases, a superintendent is not familiar with his course of study, perhaps, or is ignorant of the texts in use in his school.   He may not know even the approximate enrollment in grades or high school.   Once the author visited a superintendent of a school of ten teachers.   Two buildings were in use, a Primary building and a combination building of grades and high school.   The two buildings stood on separate lots, perhaps two hundred feet apart.   On inquiry, the superintendent, although he had been in charge of the schools all year, could not tell whether the Primary building contained inside toilets.

The above are a few illustrations of careless ignorance. A live superintendent should know more about his school than any other person does. He should know how each department is functioning; he should know which teachers are doing efficient work, and should seek to assist those who are not.

Besides knowing the inside workings of his school he should also know some outside matters, such as salaries paid, the school levy, the financial limitations of the district, etc. He should know the rules of the school and should be familiar with the school laws of his state, and the further regulations of the State Department of Public Instruction.

To be at his best, also, the superintendent should know his community. He should seek personal acquaintance with the city officials and other leading citizens. If the town supports a commercial organization he should ally himself with it in an active way. A superintendent can serve his school best who is in touch with community life. To use the words of another, "the best superintendent is the one who is 'on the job' every minute."

Home Study. A difficult task usually is the securing, on the part of students, adequate home study. In the High School and the Grammar department it is legitimate to require regular evening home study by students who cannot prepare all their work in school. It is doubtful if pupils below the Grammar department should be required to do home study.

Necessary as home study work seems to be in the upper departments of the school, there will always be difficulty in securing it from all students, owing to home conditions. The tendency to shorten the school day, therefore, is a wrong tendency. If it were possible to lengthen the school day sufficiently for all preparations to be made in the school room, under supervision of the instructors, it would seem more logical. Supervised study periods and intensive study in the school will help in the solution.

Financial Plan. As a business, the school organization is peculiar. The expense budget, consisting of interest on value of plant, overhead and operating expense is concrete, but the returns on the product are abstract and largely indefinite. There is no income from the sale of the product. But, neither is the school philanthropic in its nature, as is a church. It is more of a government institution, like a state, supported by taxation. In a way this is an advantage, since the income is definitely fixed and perfectly reliable. On the other hand, it endangers efficient management. How is a School Board or a superintendent to know whether or not the school is a financial success? There is no annual inventory taken and no debit and credit columns, no gain and loss sheets. In a way the financing of a school is apt to be haphazard. School officers work gratuitously and have their own business enterprises to care for, so cannot give school finances the care they should have. The superintendent is engaged in directing educational policies rather than in studying school finances. Therefore, school business is not only haphazard, but neglected. In such a way there must be financial waste, as in most cases there is.

While the above is the present condition, there is a remedy. Large districts may employ a paid secretary to handle finances, but small districts must depend more on the superintendent. A successful superintendent needs some training in School finance, and training schools should provide such. The budget system should be understood and applied. Monthly financial reports may be presented to the "Board", and also an annual report.

Data may be gathered from schools in regard to comparative expenditures for different items. The following table is suggestive:

1. Annual expenditure for teachers.
2. Annual expenditure for buildings and grounds (including regular annual payment on bonds and interest on bonds).
3. Annual expenditure for permanent equipment.
4. Annual expenditure for current supplies.
5. Annual expenditure for janitor service and other service, on buildings and grounds, including insurance.
6. Annual expenditure for lights, water and telephone.
7. Annual expenditure for fuel.
8. Annual expenditure for service of secretary, treasurer and for election expenses.
9. Average enrollment in
    (a) Primary Department
    (b) Intermediate Department
    (c) Grammar Department
    (d) High School Department.
10. Total teacher hire for
    (a) Primary Department
    (b) Intermediate Department
    (c) Grammar Department
    (d) High School Department.
11. Number of pupils studying special subjects and teachers employed for each.
    (a) Home Economics
    (b) Manual Training
    (c) Agriculture
    (d) Drawing
    (e) Penmanship
    (f) Vocal Music
    (g) Foreign Language.

12. Average cost of instruction per pupil in each department and each grade.

13. Average cost of instruction per subject in high school and for special subjects.

14. Percentage of school levy compared to possible total levy. How does the levy compare with other similar districts?

By questionnaire sent out, a superintendent may secure data from about twenty schools for comparison with the same data of his own school. He can thus ascertain whether his own school is above or below the average on any or all items. For best results he should select schools somewhat near the size of his own school, and scattered in different parts of the state. If the school be a rural consolidated school, questions may be added in reference to transportation of pupils, etc. By this means it will be possible for a superintendent to secure a measuring stick for financing his own school. This compared with the financial limitations of his own district in school taxation will assist him to work out a safe financial plan for his school.

CHAPTER XV

A Forward Look

Retrospect. School organization and administration has been a growth, and a rapid growth. A generation ago schools were, except in the city, simple in nature and of a loose organization. A school then could not, in other words, be called a "system" of schools, but each room or grade was largely independent of all the other rooms or grades. The nominal head of the school, usually called "the principal," was a teacher of the most advanced department and spent practically all his time in instruction. Before and after school hours he was sometimes engaged in threshing recalcitrant pupils sent to him from various rooms, but this was about the extent of his duties, either as administrator or supervisor. Not always was there even a regular course of study, a teacher being allowed to teach what she desired and whatever she thought her pupils could successfully pursue.

Developing a System. During the past thirty years there has been a rapid development of schools into a system. High schools have multiplied until every village has a high school or is ambitious to get one. Even rural communities are consolidating and establishing high schools. The establishing of a high school necessitates organization and a course of study in the grades. Co-ordination of the high school and the elementary school thus becomes necessary. This calls for careful planning and some supervision of the work. Naturally the duty of arranging the course and supervising the work falls to the head teacher of the school, the teacher of the highest grades. He is given chief charge and responsibility and takes on some supervisory work, although in the small school system he is still more instructor than supervisor.

There has come also in this period a multiplicity of subjects to be taught. Many subjects have been legislated into the school, and are therefore required. The adding of special subjects has called for special teachers for such subjects, or in the larger school systems special supervisors. All this adds to the administrative work of some one, the "principal" of the school. Because of his administrative work he takes the title, "superintendent". While he may still be instructor for several subjects, his chief duty is as administrator and supervisor. The various organizations within the school need direction, and this naturally falls to the superintendent.

The Evolution of the "Superintendent": The above paragraph suggests what the superintendent has been and where he comes from. He has come directly from the ranks of the teacher, usually from the teacher of the highest department of the particular school. He has developed by taking over functions that in the small school system the Board of Education was wont to assume, and by taking on added duties accruing to the school as it became more complex. The Board of Education in the small village today assumes duties which the "Board" in a larger system delegates to the superintendent, such as the selection of teachers. In some small schools even yet the superintendent is not asked to attend regular meetings of the Board of Education, as he should be, although in the large system he is always required to attend.

Importance of the Superintendency. The old saying "As is the teacher, so is the school," has been changed to, "As is the superintendent, so is the school." In other words, the success of the school depends largely on the ability and the faithfulness of the superintendent. The success of an individual teacher depends much on the assistance and direction rendered by the superintendent. Young teachers may be trained in service by the superintendent to become mediocre teachers or highly successful, while lack of proper supervision may render some teachers dismal failures. Even the attitude of pupils and students and their success in their work may depend upon their personal relations to the superintendent.

It is generally considered that a strong, experienced superintendent is needed in a large school system, but that almost any teacher with proper educational preparation for teaching can succeed as superintendent of a small school system. This is partly a fallacy. While it is true that many superintendents of larger schools have received their training for such position while engaged as superintendent of smaller school systems, the small system needs a capable superintendent. The school here is not so well organized and therefore needs organizing ability in the superintendent. There are many administrative and supervisory problems in the small system of schools which in the larger system may be turned over to principals and supervisors. The small school therefore **needs a competent** superintendent fully as much as does the larger school, although not necessarily one so experienced. Teachers in small school systems are not usually so well qualified nor so experienced as those in larger ones, hence the more need of assistance from a capable superintendent.

Need of Training. Mention has previously been made of the need on the part of a prospective superintendent of special training in **Administration and Supervision.**

Our universities and some of our colleges are establishing courses for just this purpose, and it is now possible for a young man or a young woman who desires to make school administration a life profession to prepare for this directly instead of passing through a long experimental period of teaching, etc.

The Prospect.   The rapid growth of school systems in villages and the numerous consolidations of rural school districts into organized graded school systems have added to the demand for competent superintendents.

The recent remarkable increase in salary for superintendent indicates that Boards of Education are appreciating more his importance.   The tendency to longer terms of office is another good indication.   A number of the better schools now employ a superintendent for a term of three years or more and pay him on the twelve-months basis.   The outlook for professionalism in the superintendency and also in the high school principalship is encouraging.   More superintendents are entering the profession as a life work.

The New Organization.   The coming superintendent must be an organizer, as well as an administrator and a supervisor; he must have business ability.   The criticism of our present school system is that it is autocratic and not flexible.   The superintendent under the present system is accused of commanding his teachers and "bossing" the pupils.   He is sometimes said to be arbitrary in dealing with patrons.   The new school system must therefore be on a different basis.   Teachers are demanding, and rightfully so, more voice in directing the affairs of the school, in arranging the curriculum, in choosing texts and material and directing the general policy of the school.   Students in the high school are clamoring for some part in direction of the high school.   Student government and student co-operation in government are being tried out by isolated schools. These movements are still in the experimental stage, but show the trend in local demand. Parent and Teacher organizations in many places are taking hold of school problems. The wise superintendent will recognize this trend and adjust his school organization accordingly. This does not mean that he shall try every theory nor adopt every fad in school organization. His plan should be to adapt rather than to adopt.

With this demand for student and teacher participation in school government, it should be remembered that it ought to affect the legislative side rather than the executive or the judicial side. In school government as well as in political government there should be one responsible administrative head. Teacher councils and student councils may have a legitimate place, but to carry out the decisions of the council the superintendency should function. It should be remembered, too, that students and even some young teachers lack experience and mature judgment to handle important matters. Co-operative student government is rather for the purpose of training than for assistance in the process of administration, and as such has an important place in the scheme of the school.

Community Leadership. In another chapter brief mention has been made of social center activities. On the part of communities there is a constantly growing demand that the public school assume social leadership. It is recognized that the school is the best agency for community center activities, and that the superintendent and his teachers are naturally, by virtue of their position, community leaders. Some boards of education require that an applicant for the position of superintendent show his ability and willingness to take direction of community matters in this way. In small towns and in rural consolidated districts this is especially important. The school of the future is destined to become a stronger factor in the community life, whether located in a rural community, a town or city.

Community Participation in Education. The school of the past has been isolated. Usually in a town the building and grounds have occupied a place on the outskirts. Pupils were therefore sent out of the town proper to do their school work. The text-book was the basis of their education. The school was not vitally connected with the stirring life of the community. Pupils were ignorant of many important things in their own community; their daily education was not connected up with illustrative material close at hand. In Economics, for instance, the subject of Division of Labor was taught from a text, when a local industry would provide a concrete example. Rules of health were learned from a text instead of local sanitation being considered first hand. In other words, local factors in education were ignored by the school.

This is now being changed. The school is coming to see the value of local educational factors and the community is awakening to its responsibility in education. Better co-operation is developing. Clean-up days are instituted whereby the pupils may have a part in rendering the community more sanitary; instead of merely reading "The Village Blacksmith", pupils now visit with the teacher a local blacksmith shop; Geography classes make field trips, and Agriculture classes spray fruit trees in the neighborhood. Local talent in business and society give talks before bodies of students. The school is called upon to participate in local celebrations, etc. At the same time, by night classes, the school is giving back to the homes some educational opportunities. Demonstrations in Home Economics, etc., are offered for the benefit of mothers and working girls.

All this has much promise in betterment of the school and betterment of the community life. At the same time it adds to the responsibility of the teacher, the principal and the superintendent, and dignifies their work. The trend toward community co-operation is doing much to professionalize the occupation of teaching, for all **professions** are based on service to the community. This exalts the position of the superintendent and honors the office of the members of the Board of Education. To accomplish its best results the school must **in its operation be placed more on a business basis** and **in its purpose be placed more on a professional basis.**